Poison-Arrow Frogs

Poison-Arrow Frogs

Their Natural History and Care in Captivity

RALF HESELHAUS

Translated by Astrid Mick

BLANDFORD

Blandford
An imprint of Cassell,
Villiers House, 41/47 Strand, London WC2N 5JE

First published in the UK 1992

Distributed in Australia by
Capricorn Link (Australia) Pty Ltd.
PO Box 665, Lane Cove, NSW 2066

British Library Cataloguing in Publication Data
Heselhaus, Ralf
  Poison-Arrow frogs.
  1. Frogs
  I. Title   II. [Pfeilgift Frosche. *English*]
  597.89

  ISBN 0-7137-2257-6

Translated from the German by Astrid Mick
Printed and bound in Great Britain
by Mackays of Chatham

Contents

Acknowledgements 7

Preface 9

Taxonomy – A Brief Note 11

1 Where Do They Live? 13

2 Expedition to Panama 15

3 Expedition to French Guiana 23

4 Fearsomely Poisonous 29

5 Belligerent Pugilists 32

6 Survival Artists 34

7 The Unique Frog Parent 36

8 Care in the Terrarium 38

9 Successful Breeding in Captivity 53

10 The Genus *Dendrobates* 56

11 The Genus *Phyllobates* 81

12 The Genus *Colostethus* 100

Bibliography 108

Index 111

Acknowledgements

I would like to thank the original publisher, Eugen Ulmer, for making this beautifully illustrated book possible.

Matthias Schmidt of Münster made valuable contributions throughout and my especial thanks are due to him for editing the chapter 'Expedition to French Guiana'. I must thank also Dr Heinz Wermuth of Freiberg for reading and editing the manuscript, and Frank Klusener of Münster and Manfred Salewski of Dinslaken for their help in producing several photos.

The preparation of the English-language edition was greatly helped by the work of the translator, Astrid Mick, and by the advice given by Chris Mattison, Professor Malcolm Peaker and Jerry Cole.

Picture Credits
All photos are by Ralf Heselhaus apart from 27 (Lothar Bindewald), 49 (Hilmar Hansen) and 62 (Matthias Schmidt).

Line illustrations are by Karin Aichele.

Preface

Poison-arrow or poison-dart frogs – the Dendrobatidae – are now among the most popular animals kept in terraria. Because of their unusual behaviour and impressive form of parental care, these little frogs, which are so colourful that they look as if they had been lacquered or varnished, are fascinating to not only experienced terrarium keepers but also beginners.

In the opening chapters of this book, the inexperienced enthusiast will find a useful introduction to the world of poison-arrow frogs, including facts about their habitat and the way they care for their young. Although *Phyllobates terribilis*, the 'terrible poison frog', is the most venomous animal in the world – South American Indians use toxins from its skin for their deadly blow-pipe arrows – handling successive generations of its offspring bred in a terrarium becomes progressively less risky, because over time these creatures almost cease to produce toxins. The care and breeding of poison-arrow frogs will be explained in detail, so that even the beginner, if committed, will be able to breed these climbers of trees and leaves successfully.

Again and again over the last few years, new subspecies and colour variations of the poison-arrow frog have been found. The frogs seem to enjoy an almost infinite range of shape and colour, continually presenting scientists with difficult problems of nomenclature. To the enthusiast, however, there are no problems here: every new variation is a treat.

This new work contains completely up-to-date information on the whole range of poison-arrow frogs, taking into account a number of new species. It describes and depicts some 50 of the presently known 65 species of *Dendrobates* and *Phyllobates*, so all the species important for breeding in terraria are covered.

In conclusion, I would like to comment on the current laws governing protected species. These should be amended by the relevant authorities so that they can make a true contribution towards the protection of species. Bans and limitations on keeping animals are not enough, by themselves, to protect endangered species and ensure their survival, but committed keepers of terraria are perhaps in a position to make a valuable contribution by breeding animals for their survival.

Ralf Heselhaus

Taxonomy – A Brief Note

Taxonomy, right at the beginning? Perhaps that seems a bit dry, but we are not going to manage completely without it. If you want to understand poison-arrow frogs, you have to be able to distinguish between the individual species, familiarize yourself with the different genera and acquire a rough overview of the frog's position in the animal kingdom.

The class of Amphibia, into which all amphibian animals have been placed, was first introduced by the Swedish naturalist Linnaeus in 1758. Further refinements of his system by Boulenger in 1878 and Noble in 1931 have led to today's system of nomenclature, which gives all animals their scientific names. The name of a species consists of two words and that of a subspecies of three words. The first is the name of the genus, the second that of the species and the third, where there is one, that of the subspecies.

So, let us take, for example, the strawberry poison-arrow frog, *Dendrobates pumilio*. We know, first of all, that it belongs to the class of Amphibia. Anciently, amphibians were the first vertebrates to evolve air-breathing lungs and they conquered the land. But, unlike the reptiles and more highly evolved vertebrates, amphibians were unable to abandon the water completely. It is true of the great majority of amphibians that each individual has to pass through a larval stage in water before becoming a land creature at a later, advanced stage of development.

Amphibia are divided into three groups or orders – the tailed amphibians (Caudata), the jumping amphibians (Anura) and the Gymnophiona. Of these, the order Anura, which encompasses frogs, is by far the most successful: it comprises about 2,600 species in approximately 250 genera – there are almost ten times more species of frog than there are of tailed amphibians (Caudata). The strawberry poison-arrow frog belongs to the order of Anura. Within that order, it belongs to the family Denrobatidae, the poison-arrow frogs.

This family consists of about 135 species. There is still controversy surrounding classification into the three genera *Dendrobates*, *Phyllobates* and *Colostethus*. Myers (1983) includes in the family a fourth genus, *Atopophrynus*, which is represented by one single species. A revised classification by Silverstone (1975a, 1976) lists about 20 *Dendrobates* and 20 *Phyllobates* species. According to more recent views (Myers *et al.*, 1978), the following species listed by Silverstone as *Phyllobates*, should belong to the genus *Dendrobates*: *anthonyi, bassleri, bolivianus, boulengerie-espinosai, femoralis, ingeri, parvulus, pictus, petersi, pulchripectus, smaragdinus, tricolor, trivittatus* and *zaparo*.

Including newly described species, 65 species of the two genera *Dendrobates* and *Phyllobates* are known today. In addition, there are at least 70 species in the genus *Colostethus*.

I have based the taxonomy of poison-arrow frogs in this book on Silverstone's revision (1975a, 1976), as Myers's version has not yet been universally accepted. For all those species to which some taxonomic ambiguity applies, I have added in brackets the generic description *Dendrobates* (following Myers *et al.*, 1978) after the classification according to Silverstone.

1
Where Do They Live?

Poison-arrow frogs are at home in the warm and humid rain forests of South and Central America and in the southern areas of Central America. There, where everything is steaming with heat and moisture, and the sun can penetrate the dense green of jungle trees and reach the ground only with difficulty, we find them, hopping and climbing by day through the foliage and over tree stumps.

Poison-arrow frogs live in those parts of the world we generally term the tropics, where there is much sunlight and temperatures are high, with only minor variations, all the year round. There, too, an immense range of small insects is available for food. Because of the toxins in their skin, poison-arrow frogs have protection against predators and it might be thought that they could therefore pursue their daily activities in peace, in almost paradisaical conditions, but even they are involved in a daily battle for survival. They have to cope with torrential downpours, which to a small frog must seem of flood-like proportions, and they also have to watch out for predators, which still view them as delicate morsels in spite of their toxic skins. Certainly not all of these frogs are so toxic as to be able to spoil the appetites of their enemies.

Although they live in a very homogeneous climate, with temperatures seldom falling below 20°C and rarely rising above 30°C, poison-arrow frogs inhabit a range of different small environments. Some species – for example, the false poison-arrow frog (*Colostethus*) – live beside watercourses and, at any sign of danger, leap head first into the water to hide under leaves or stones. Other species, on the other hand, live far away from water and make do with small puddles left behind after the almost daily rain.

Some inventive species, such as the small yellow-and-black-striped *Dendrobates quinquevittatus*, have discovered mini-ponds for themselves high up in the trees. They live in the water-filled leafy funnels, or vases, of bromeliad plants, and were found by Bechter (1982) at heights of up to almost 4 m (13 ft).

The majority of these species live in warm, moist valleys, but some inhabit the cooler mountainous forests. Schulte (1979) found *Dendrobates silverstonei* in the mountain forests of the Cordillera Azul in Peru at heights of up to 1,700 m (5,500 ft). Temperatures measured there in April were 18°C (water) and 22°C (air).

Although poison-arrow frogs are generally found in a moist environment, some species inhabit areas that are seemingly dry but where low vegetation provides enough shade to keep the ground moist. Thus, there are definite differences among the species with respect to climatic requirements and lifestyles. Such differences have to be taken into consideration in the care of these frogs.

2

Expedition to Panama

Dendrobates auratus of Taboga

Panama is the Promised Land for enthusiasts of the splendid poison-arrow frogs of the Dendrobatidae family. These small diurnal frogs, which are impressive not only for their gorgeous colouring but also for their fascinating behaviour, inhabit the country in great numbers. A ramble through their natural habitat is an unforgettable adventure.

In spite of its small size – only about 800 km (500 m) long east to west – Panama is very varied geographically and climatically. The Central Cordillera, a chain of mountains running parallel to the coast whose highest point is the volcano Barú at 3,475 m (11,400 ft), divides Panama into an Atlantic and a Pacific side. While the Pacific half, apart from the inaccessible areas of the Serrania del Darien, appears clear of vegetation and is relatively dry – with the exception of a rainy period during what are in the northern hemisphere the summer months – the rainy Atlantic side is almost completely covered with impenetrable jungle. On a trip to Panama, I and my friend Matthias Schmidt, got to know these very different climatic zones.

It was a spontaneous decision to forsake a cold, wet German winter for the sweaty heat of Panama. I had, of course, often thought of visiting the home of our poison-arrow frogs, but it had been just a dream – until my friend arrived back from a trip to Panama. He had experienced much, and seen more, and desperately wanted to return. This time, though, I was determined not to let him travel alone. In no time at all, and much faster than he had anticipated, his second trip to Panama had been arranged.

The year 1986 began with a lot of excitement. On 2 January we found ourselves in the middle of hectic Panama City. Our destination was the bathing-resort island of Taboga, which can be reached by ferry from Panama City in less than an hour.

There was hardly even time to enjoy the view of Panama City's skyline during the crossing. The capital is still visible when you land on beautiful Taboga. Across the yachting harbour we could see a small village hidden among the dense greenery of the slopes. We felt in holiday mood, but we left the fine sand of the bathing beaches behind and made our way to the forest, where we hoped to find our *Dendrobates auratus*. We climbed a firm, hard forest path to reach a few places where Matthias had found the attractive golden-green *D. auratus* the year before. He was surprised how dry the forest seemed compared to his last visit during the rainy period. Standing in a hollow in which I was unable to find even a puddle, he exclaimed, 'We stood here last time wearing rubber boots, almost up to our knees in water!' The dried-up bed of a stream was the only evidence now that it might look quite different here during the rainy season.

We decided to return and start our search in another place. In the heat before noon, we climbed up through the village until we reached the forest. 'Here, in August, *Dendrobates auratus* was sitting about everywhere,' Matthias remarked drily – as dry almost as the leaves lying on the floor of the forest.

A little higher up we came upon a small rubbish tip, a promising habitat for the frogs we hoped to see. And, indeed, a short distance in front of us hopped a metallic brown-green jewel of a frog. It leapt over a sack of rubbish and disappeared inside a rusty tin can. Got him! we thought. Unfortunately, though, the can had no bottom and the little frog – only some 2 cm (¾ in) in length – was now sitting somewhere under the rubbish. We decided to continue our search in a less malodorous place. What we needed to find was water. To the left of our path, the ground-covering vegetation suddenly showed a rich shade of green; further down flowed a cheerful little stream, bubbling refreshingly over stones and tree roots.

'There's one sitting right here!' cried Matthias. With that he had already netted our first poison-arrow frog. I looked through my camera lens at this *D. auratus* habitat – ground-covering philodendra with dark-green, pointed leaves, light-green ferns and a little stream forming small pools between stones and tree roots.

Beside me, something was rustling in the leaves. Half-covered by low-growing plants, sitting amid the foliage, was a creature that usually provokes disgust and fear – a bird spider. It was comfortably settling its furry body down among the leaves, but because I wanted to photograph it, I poked it out with a stick. Including its widely spread legs, it was as big as a human hand – an impressive sight compared to its smaller relatives. But, after all, we were more interested in frogs.

The first thing we noticed was that *D. auratus* spends its time rather hidden away during dry periods. Only once did we see a frog hopping openly across a path. Most of the frogs sat near or in moist rock crevices, out of our reach. Nevertheless, we managed to catch a few. Finally, we were searching only for especially attractive examples, those that had a net-like pattern rather than the usual spotted markings of *D. auratus*. Obviously these frogs were rare among the population, as it took us well over two hours to find three specimens. Still, we were quite satisfied with the day's results as we made our way back.

Rocket Frogs of El Valle

Less than 100 km (60 m) from Panama City lies the mountain valley El Valle, our next destination. Beyond San Carlos we left the Panamerican Highway behind us and headed for the Cordillera de Talamanca. For about half an hour we drove through a landscape of cleared grazing land, then slowly we began to climb. The low hills around us looked yellow and dried up, and it took an effort of imagination to envisage the lush jungle landscape that must have existed here before huge areas of forest clearance had taken over.

The higher we climbed into the mountains, the greener everything became. It was a good road on which we made easy progress, reaching El Valle by early evening. The valley is a well-known resort in Panama, so it was not difficult to find a suitable hotel for the night.

Early next morning we carried on. We left the village behind and drove up the serpentine roads along the mountain slopes. In the ravines we saw the mountain streams flowing down to the valleys where we hoped to find the rocket frogs of the genus *Colostethus*. We drove along a narrow mountain path parallel to the course of a stream and wound down the car windows to locate the frogs by their sounds. It did not take long for us to pick out the typical whistling of *Colostethus* from the surrounding tropical background noises. As we climbed out of the car we were greeted by such a noisy frog concert that any doubts were ruled out – we were standing in the middle of the rocket frog's habitat. All we had to do was grab them. But in the event catching these little frogs proved to be far more difficult than we had assumed in our initial euphoria.

We ran down to the mountain stream, which gushed along idyllically over rocks and fallen tree trunks, and then understood why *Colostethus* keep up this penetrating whistling sound – they have no other way of making themselves heard over the loudly rushing waters. Suddenly, silence. At a stroke all the frog noises had ceased. We could not see a single frog. Somewhere in among the flat, partly submerged rocks, the little fellows had to be sitting!

We kept still and waited. Then, suddenly, it all began again with renewed gusto. A loud whistling, from hundreds of frog throats, filled the air. And at last we caught sight of one of these persistent little callers. In front of us, on a stone, squatted a little brown froglet, his white vocal sacs moving up and down. We crept closer carefully and took photos. We must have got too near, for suddenly he leapt into the water, allowed himself to drift with the current for a while, and then climbed out again on to a nearby rock.

A little later we saw a female *Colostethus inguinalis* hopping along, hurrying across the rocks with her offspring on her back. We managed to catch her. Her whole back was covered with completely motionless larvae – we counted thirty of them. After taking a few photos we let her hop away, so that she could set down the larvae between the stones in one of the small, quiet water pools, as is usual with this species. All around the edges of these pools we found clutches of *C. inguinalis* eggs, which had been deposited on the smooth stones under a layer of foliage. The pools themselves contained tadpoles in various stages of development. The water was relatively cool, at a temperature of 22°C. After we had managed to catch one of these frogs, which zip about as fast as rockets, we decided to make our way back. As we were returning to the car, a tiny frog, only about 1 cm (³⁄₈ in) long, hopped into the leaves at our feet. It was, as we realized when we had caught it, a *D. minutus*, which is among the tiniest of the Dendrobatidae, reaching only 1.5 cm (⁵⁄₈ in) in length. Of course, we forgot all about returning and decided instead to hunt for more examples of *D. minutus*.

As it turned out, the species was quite common along the river banks and edges of the nearby forest. However, because of its diminutive size and its plain, brown colouring, it is quite difficult to find. Its camouflage colouring renders it almost invisible among the leaves on the ground – we managed to find one only when it happened to move or jump away. Very often these little *Dendrobates* disappeared so quickly into the foliage, under tree roots or into rock crevices that we could hardly follow them with our eyes. The number of frogs we managed to outwit and capture for our terraria at home was correspondingly meagre. In the meantime it was late afternoon and we realized it was high time we returned to our hotel.

Strawberry poison-arrow frogs of the Bocas Islands

The sun was high in the sky, although it was still early morning. In our chartered motor boat, we were heading for Shepard Island, which we could make out in the distance. The Caribbean Sea lay before us, as smooth as a mirror. We reached our destination quite quickly. Shepard is one of the Bocas Islands, off the west coast of Panama, and we had come to see its unique population of strawberry poison-arrow frogs (*D. pumilio*). This island, like all the islands of the Bocas group, is hilly and covered in dense vegetation.

We climbed up the slopes used for cattle grazing, and arrived in open woodland. Great, gnarled, deciduous trees, standing apart from each other, had covered the ground with a thick layer of dead leaves. The heat and the many exotic plants growing on the branches of trees reminded us that we were indeed deep in the tropics.

Then our attention was caught by some very characteristic sounds – loud 'app-app-app' calls that could only have been made by strawberry poison-arrow frogs. Although the calls ceased as we approached, at least we now knew where to look. We saw our first olive-green strawberry poison-arrow frog perched on a tree root, but unfortunately a quick jump took it into the leaves covering the ground and it disappeared from sight.

After some futile attempts we succeeded in catching a few of these attractive little frogs. They were about 2 cm (¾ in) long and had olive-green backs and yellow-green flanks. Most were single-coloured, but some showed a delicate pattern of black dots on their backs.

While I was still looking at the frogs we had caught, Matthias shouted enthusiastically, 'Here's an *auratus!*' And there it was, a glowing, light-green frog sitting quite upright on a dead leaf on the ground – a wonderful sight. We were able to catch it, and on looking at it more closely we found that it was not entirely light green – it had a few bluish markings, especially on its head. It was 4 cm (1½ in) long.

Our search for more specimens was not very successful. *D. auratus* seemed not as frequent on Shepard as *D. pumilio*, and because it is inclined to live in hiding it is difficult to find. Finally, though, we had one interesting sighting – we watched a pair that was obviously occupied with preparations for mating. The frogs were sitting close together under a mossy fallen tree trunk, the female recognizable by its larger girth. The smaller male was croaking quietly. Just as we were about to photograph this pretty scene both animals disappeared into a hollow stump.

By now it was getting late, and we left Shepard to go back to Colon, deciding to postpone our visit to the island of Bastimentos until the following day. Next morning we started out early so as to have plenty of time for a frog hunt on Bastimentos. It took us only a quarter of an hour by boat. As Matthias already knew where to look, we headed straight through the small settlement and turned off on to a muddy path that wound its way through coconut palms back to the coast. Already I could see a few red strawberry poison-arrow frogs hopping away on either side of the path, but Matthias remarked dismissively that I need not bother about these. Finally we arrived at our goal. The frog population we were seeking inhabits a strip along the coast between coconut palms and small banana plantations. Between the palms are large fields of Araceae (*Xanthosma violaceum*). These plants offer ideal living-conditions for the small frogs, which, in the absence of other funnel-shaped plants, lay their eggs in the smooth, long, water-filled, funnelled leaves.

Our first red strawberry poison-arrow frog was sitting high up in a pile of harvested coconut shells. Perched on a half-shell, he was defending his territory with loud 'apping' calls against equally loud neighbouring competition. His vocal sacs were swelling up like balloons and his calls caused his whole body to vibrate. As we were unable to see any bromeliads in the area we assumed that the water-filled empty coconut shells served the frogs as breeding ponds for their larvae.

Gradually we discovered more and more of these glowing, metallic-red froglets hopping and climbing over the ground and on tree trunks and leaves. In the neighbouring banana plantation they appeared to be as numerous as among the coconut palms. Enthusiastically, I grabbed my camera and tried to capture the many colour forms. I photographed large frogs that were spotted red with white stomachs, orange with small dots, beige-white, yellow-green, yellow, and mixed varieties in all shades of colour. Each frog looked different! In the end I realized it would be impossible to photograph all the many different varieties. To arrive at some kind of general conclusion about the distribution of the various colour combinations we would have to adopt a systematic procedure. So we counted the frogs we had collected. The results showed that red and orange frogs predominated – they made up about 90 per cent of the population. The remaining 10 per cent consisted of frogs of other colours, white to yellow being fairly frequent. Chocolate-brown strawberry frogs and single-coloured frogs with no pattern of spots were very rare.

With its huge number of differently coloured forms, *D. pumilio* of the Bocas Islands has become an interesting subject of scientific research. How to explain the enormous variability of this species? At first, experts assumed that the geological development of Panama should be seen as the cause for the variety of strawberry poison-arrow frogs on the Bocas Islands. At the end of the last Ice Age, about 12,000 years ago, the islands of the Bocas archipelago were separated from the mainland by rising sea levels. Because of this long separation, different island varieties could have evolved, as has happened many times during the course of evolution with other species of animals. However, the separation theory alone cannot explain the profusion of forms of *D. pumilio*. On the island of Bastimentos especially, one coherent population contains all the vast variety that this frog displays.

Bearing this in mind, we have to accept that a long separation of populations, together with specialization and mutation, cannot be the only reason for this profusion. It appears that the gene pool of the species *D. pumilio* is so inventive that it produces ever-new colours and patterns. Even more astonishing is the fact that individual colour forms are not only visibly different but differ also in their behaviour and breeding patterns. The red and orange frogs are especially bold, while the brown and yellow frogs seem rather shy. In the choice of egg-laying sites and mating behaviour also there are differences specific to populations. Finally, many colour forms differ in the composition of their skin toxin.

We are perhaps observing on the Bocas Islands a golden age in the evolution of strawberry poison-arrow frogs, which is presently expressing unlimited possibilities in ever-new colour forms. This is not happening because of an evolutionary 'whim' of nature, but in order to 'invent' the best-adapted strawberry poison-arrow frog with the most chances of survival because, of course, all the possible predators of *D. pumilio* are also continuing to evolve, and habitats can change. The strawberry poison-arrow frog, however, is well prepared. As the most varied species in the world, it is sure to win the battle for survival at least in one of its varieties.

3
Expedition to French Guiana

At home in Germany I had already prepared myself intensively for this trip. After a great number of phone calls to French Guiana my date of departure had been fixed. I had been waiting for a long time, ready for a flight out, when from the other end of the line came the message, 'Il pleut.' It was raining, giving the best possible conditions for my search for poison-arrow frogs. A quick dash to the travel agent to book my flight and four days later there I and a friend were in the middle of the jungle.

In Search of *Dendrobates quinquevittatus*

We left our hotel early in the morning, in order to be at the frogs' habitat by sunrise. We set off in a hired car, crossed the River Comté by ferry, then carried on along a jungle road towards Camp Caiman, a small hostel along the way. The further we went the worse the road became. Every few minutes a deluge of rainwater descended, as though a bathtub had been emptied over us. Every so often visibility fell to zero and I had to stop the car. I checked the route directions I had been given. This had to be our destination, hadn't it? Perhaps not. Everything looked so dauntingly alike.

Rubber boots, compass, torches, machetes and containers for our catch – we had thought of everything. We slashed our way through the edge of the vegetation, which luckily was fairly sparse, disturbing a snake (*Bothrops atrox*) in the process, and there we were in the middle of the jungle. Again we realized how many potential dangers lurk there. It was not only the snakes, which startled us on numerous occasions, reminding us of the respect that should be accorded them. It was also that in such unknown, pathless territory it is easy to get lost – and that could be dangerous. It is important to mark your path so that you can find your way back. If all else failed, we at least had our compass.

After more than an hour's walking we arrived at the entrance to a small cave. We dug out our torches and, keeping them handy, crawled in. Just a short way inside we disturbed thousands of bats, which flew from the cave in their excitement. We ducked and covered our faces with our hands. There seemed to be more and more bats. The beating of their wings filled the cave with a strange background sound. There was so little room that they kept brushing against us. Finally we reached a larger, vault-like cave where we were able to stand upright again. In the light of our torches we picked out a number of bats of the species *Bufo marinus*. These shared the roof of the cave with spiders as big as the palm of the hand.

This excursion, although fascinating, was a fruitless one. We had been side-tracked, so we left the cave and made our way back to the car, where I checked again with the directions for finding the place where we hoped to find the frogs. We had been told that if we found bromeliads we would find frogs, because they make their homes in almost every sort of ground-covering bromeliad. But up until now we had not seen a single one. We drove on and tried our luck in a different place. Again, we were unsuccessful. Our search for *D. quinquevittatus* was proving to be a lot more difficult than we had thought at first – we had been travelling for several days now and had not found a single frog. Then, on the fourth day we discovered a place that gave us fresh hope. Here were bromeliads that seemed to provide suitable homes for frogs – pineapple plants. Carefully we searched through the thorn. There! A *D. quinquevittatus*, not even half-grown, hopped cheekily towards us. Unfortunately, this was the only one we could find – a long and intensive search uncovered no more specimens. They had to be somewhere, but where? And where were the bromeliads? It seemed that the fields of bromeliads, which had been so numerous not so long ago, had been destroyed, and along with them the habitat of *D. quinquevittatus*. I had had similar experiences in Panama, where different populations of *D. pumilio* had been forced to find alternative habitats. So from then on we extended our search to different kinds of habitat. The forest became less dense and the ground cover more lush; it was filled with the croaking, or, to be exact, the trilling, of many types of frog. I was sure that I could hear a *D. femoralis*. But whenever we drew close to one of these frog concerts, silence would descend. Hours passed without our seeing even a single frog. Then, suddenly, right in front of my foot, a small dark-brown animal darted across the leaves. I turned back one leaf after the other, and at last saw before me a poison-arrow frog – a *D. femoralis*. Before I could net it, it escaped with fast, long leaps and I set out in pursuit. Suddenly something fell on my neck from the branches above. Without thinking, I turned my head and found myself looking directly into the eyes of a green snake about a metre long. I think we were both paralysed with shock. After a few seconds the snake dived into my shirt, wriggled through my sleeve and landed in a bush to my right. When I had got over my feeling of revulsion, I had a better look at it. It was a false adder, *Oxybelis fulgidus*. Like me, it seemed to have plucked up its courage, and with a wide-open mouth it darted again and again at my outstretched hand. After about a minute, the game was over and it disappeared into the undergrowth.

Shortly afterwards I heard a quiet rasping coming from above my head. I located the sound in a banana plant, and there I spied, sitting in a curled leaf, a resting male of the species *D. quinquevittatus*. I found the female of the pair no more than 30 cm away. Success at last! After this, I began to concentrate my search on banana plantations and philodendron stands. Unfortunately, these were not very common, although I did manage to find quite a few more frogs.

I found that although *D. quinquevittatus* can climb to the very top of a banana plant it will equally happily live near the ground. Noticeably, it is the female that seems to prefer to be lower down and the male that prefers a regular perch higher up. As a rule these little yellow-striped frogs live together in pairs in quite a large territory. Occasionally I have found up to 10 frogs in one banana plant. Water reservoirs in the leaf axils serve in the same way as do bromeliad vases, as nurseries for the young.

All in all, watching these little frogs in their natural habitat was a fascinating experience. I shall remember the first *D. quinquevittatus* we discovered in the wild for a long time.

'Islands' of *Dendrobates tinctorius*

The coastal areas of French Guiana are wide marshlands from which occasional low hills, higher hills and chains of mountains rise. These, with an average height of 100–200 m (300–650 ft), provide an ideal environment for *D. tinctorius*.

Our first excursion was to a small hill quite near Cayenne. Friends had told me that here I might still find some white *D. tinctorius* with a fine reticulated pattern.

Viewed from the road, this did not seem a hopeful-looking environment. It was an island encirled by roads. The vegetation at its edges was decorated with rubbish. None the less we ploughed through into the interior of the forest. It was very dark here – only a tiny amount of light reaches the ground. At intervals of about 50 m (160 ft) small, bizarrely shaped rock formations rose from the ground. Roots covered the stony ground. Various kinds of creeper sprawled over the rocks, which were considerably eroded by rainwater. Everywhere small water reservoirs had formed, offering excellent conditions for the tadpoles of the frogs we were seeking. And soon we found a tadpole almost at the point of metamorphosis, already clearly displaying white back-markings. We carried on with our search for the frogs themselves, but hours passed before we finally found two specimens of these beautiful but quite shy frogs. They have dark-blue or black legs and black backs with numerous white dots. Unfortunately, it proved to be very difficult to sex this colour form – the differences are hard to see.

Probably the best-known form of *D. tinctorius* from French Guiana is the yellow type. After much tedious searching we found these frogs on the slopes of a mountain in the north-western part of the country. The leafy ceiling of the forest is formed by the tops of giant jungle trees, covered in epiphytes, and only a very little daylight reaches the rather sparse vegetation of the relatively dry floor of the forest. We were able to ramble across this terrain without much difficulty and soon found what we were looking for. The frogs' strongly coloured markings practically shone out at us. Very often they sat a short way up, motionless against the smooth trunks of the jungle giants upon which their territories are centred. The small cracks and clefts in the trunks provide permanent reservoirs of water and are ideal places for depositing their eggs. Sometimes we would see the frogs sitting about 10 m (30 ft) up, on almost vertical surfaces. The number inhabiting any one tree would depend on the circumference of the trunk and the arrangement of its huge, spreading roots. Really large trees can accommodate as many as five frogs. As a rule, *D. tinctorius* lives in pairs. As the sex of the yellow form was fairly easy to determine – by body size and the larger fingertips of the male – we were able to establish that never more than two males lived together in one tree home.

The frogs were active throughout the day, but they left their tree to look for food only for short periods. When we investigated their forest habitat more closely we never found a single *D. tinctorius* specimen more than 5 m (15 ft) from its tree.

We found that the frogs were present in large numbers only in an area of some 300 × 100 m (900 × 300 ft). There seemed to be no particular reason why this should be so, but beyond this area these beautiful frogs seemed to have disappeared from the face of the earth and were rarely to be found.

We had soon explored the few roads of French Guiana and to locate further territories of *D. tinctorius* we had now to turn to boats and helicopters.

A chartered helicopter took us to the extreme east of the country, close to the Brazilian border. We flew over huge swamps that are home to caymans. It is awe-inspiring to see so many of these animals, up to 4.5 m (15 ft) long, still in such great numbers.

We flew over low hillocks jutting at almost regular intervals out of the swamps – the 'islands' of *D. tinctorius*. We landed on one of these unusual 'islands' and set up camp. The helicopter departed – from now on we were on our own. We left our camp site at dawn so as to make the most of the time at our disposal. Great clouds of mosquitoes were our constant companions. We walked through giant fields of bromeliads – pineapple plant after pineapple plant grew here. Unfortunately, this was a dry period, and consequently the poison-arrow frogs we were seeking spent their time hidden away. It was several hours before we found our first frogs, but then each one seemed more beautiful than the last! The dark blue to black of their backs is broken up by large white patches and their flanks are almost completely white.

This area differed from the other environments we had seen in that the terrain was not rocky and there were no great jungle trees. The colouring of this form of *D. tinctorius* is associated only with frogs dwelling on the ground amid profuse bromeliads. It is to be assumed, therefore, that every large jungle 'island' offers a home to its own form of *D. tinctorius*. I am certain that it cannot be long before new forms and perhaps even new species are discovered.

After three days in the jungle we heard the helicopter approaching and were ready for our return to the capital. Successful, and richer by many experiences and adventures, we left the 'islands' of *D. tinctorius*.

4
Fearsomely Poisonous

Poison-arrow frogs are looked upon as the Borgias of the amphibians. All members of the Dendrobatidae family, without distinction, have been condemned as 'murderers' or 'poisoners'. But new investigations have revealed an altogether different picture. In the early 1970s Charles W. Myers, John W. Daly and Boris Malkin caught a frog that contained a truly fearsome quantity of toxic substance – enough to kill about 20,000 mice or, on another scale, 10 humans. This new species was promptly and aptly named *Phyllobates terribilis*. But at about the same time it was shown that other species were much less toxic than had previously been assumed. It had also been the prevailing opinion until then that the frogs with the most glowing colours were the most poisonous. But this view is no longer held. The highly toxic *P. terribilis* is a rather unassuming yellow, while some species with very conspicuous colouring – for example, the intense red *D. silverstonei* – are not overly toxic. Schulte (1979) noted that Indian women had observed that *D. silverstonei* is often pecked at, and even eaten by, hens. Investigations by Myers and Daly (1979) showed that this species actually deploys only a relatively small quantity of toxin, which contains neither any of the steroid-batrachotoxins nor the highly poisonous pumiliotoxin B. Its main constituents are alkaloids of the pumiliotoxin groups A and C. But we are dealing here with extremely complicated chemical compounds, which could be analysed only very recently, and which still pose many unsolved puzzles.

The most toxic of these coloured frogs, according to Myers and Daly (1983a), are the three *Phyllobates* species which live west of the Andes, in the Pacific river areas of Colombia – *P aurotaenia*, *P. bicolor* and *P. terribilis*. Their toxin is even more potent than the notorious plant poison curare.

The Chocó Indians of Colombia use the skin secretions of these species in the preparation of their blow-pipe arrows. In northern Colombia the Indians still obtain this poison in the way described by Captain Charles Stuart Cochrane over 160 years ago. Cochrane explored Colombia in 1823–4 and the Spaniards there showed him *rana de veneno* (poison frogs) which were 'about three inches long and had yellow backs and very large black eyes'.

Cochrane reported: 'Those who use this toxin catch the frogs in the forests and then keep them in a piece of hollow sugar cane, feeding them regularly until they are needed for their poison. Then the Indians fish this unhappy amphibian out and impale it with a sharp stick, which they push down the frog's gullet until it emerges at its back legs. This ordeal makes the poor frog begin to sweat, especially on its back, which becomes covered in white foam. This foam is the most effective toxin produced by the frog. Into it the Indians dip the tips of their arrows, which then retain their lethal properties for a whole year.'

The southern Chaco Indians, on the other hand, whose territory is the habitat of *P. terribilis*, do not have to maltreat 'their' poison frog in this fashion. Because *P. terribilis* is so highly toxic, it is quite sufficient simply to pass arrowheads across the back of a live specimen.

Poison-arrow frogs produce their poison in toxin-secreting glands of the skin, the so-called granular glands. The minute openings of these glands are dispersed among the openings of mucous glands, which in turn are distributed over the entire surface of a frog's skin. The glands become active as soon as the frog is subject to stress. A predator carrying a poison frog in its mouth will feel either a burning sensation, a numb feeling or a disagreeable taste, and quickly drop its prey. (This applies mainly to the highly toxic species – some, as we have said, are not nearly as toxic as their bold warning colours would seem to signal.)

Toxins are not used merely for the purpose of frightening off predators. They also prevent bacteria and fungi from colonizing the frog's permanently moist skin, where they would find ideal conditions for multiplying.

On the whole, it is best not to try to keep the three highly toxic species *P. aurotenia*, *P. bicolor* and, especially, *P. terribilis* in a terrarium. The skin secretions of these species include batrachotoxins, which are among the most powerful of non-protein toxins. Handling these frogs, therefore, requires a great deal of caution. The highly poisonous batrachotoxin is a nerve toxin. It creates an irreversible blocking of the ends of the axons (nerve fibres) of motor neurons if a sufficient dose enters the blood stream. Death results through muscular and respiratory paralysis. According to Myers and Daly (1983a), handling *P. terribilis* can be dangerous even if you just hold the frog in your hand. (The poison is perhaps absorbed through the pores of the skin?) Handling the other species, however, should be safe enough. In principle, though, it is best to avoid handling poison-arrow frogs. When catching a frog, or transferring it from one terrarium to another, I have found it useful to allow it to hop into a small plastic tube – but this is to spare it unnecessary stress rather than to protect the handler from toxins. Should you have to handle the frogs at any time, it goes without saying that you should wash your hands thoroughly afterwards.

Experience in handling poison-arrow frogs has demonstrated that they lose a great deal of their toxicity after a lengthy period in a terrarium. For years I have kept poison-arrow frogs accustomed to a terrarium side by side with tree frogs (*Hyla*) and with geckos (*Phelsuma*), without suffering any losses. I have seen a *H. ebraccata* jump on top of a *D. pumilio* when startled and a gecko lick a *P. tricolor*. Neither encounter seemed to have had any detrimental consequences.

Newly imported animals, on the other hand, because of stress situations during capture and transport, have usually accumulated a considerably greater quantity of toxins in their mucous membranes. Matthias Schmidt told me that *D. tinctorius* freshly imported from Surinam exuded a whitish slime which, when he picked one up, gave him a definite burning sensation in the palm of his hand. After acclimatizing, the frogs no longer manifested this secretion.

The proper handling of poison-arrow frogs should preclude any danger of human poisoning. But *P. terribilis* is best left in its tropical home, where the Indians have a greater need of it than we do.

5

Belligerent Pugilists

Two small, red-and-white-striped froglets (*P. tricolor*) are sitting facing each other on the ground. Both are straining to appear as tall as possible, front legs splayed out and rigid. They are like knights at a tournament. As if responding to some invisible signal, they leap simultaneously at one another with a whistling battle cry. They clash, then embrace, standing upright on their hindlegs for a fraction of a second, looking like boxers in a ring. They circle one another, then come together again. Each tries to get behind his opponent so that he can jump on his back and press him to the ground, but neither creature will yield and the battle ends in a draw.

In spite of its small size the poison-arrow frog is no pacifist. Its territory is sacrosanct, and woe betide the intruder who does not respect its boundaries.

It is usually males that display this territorial behaviour and insist on their rights to a certain territory. But the females of some species also behave aggressively towards both members of their own species and other frogs.

Poison-arrow frogs do not show fair play in defending their territories. You can sometimes get unpleasant surprises if you keep several males of one or more species together. Zimmermann (1978) noticed several unusual deaths in a terrarium stocked with three *D. pumilio* and 10 almost fully grown *P. lugubris*. At short intervals he found several drowned *P. lugubris* in the terrarium's water basin. Then he saw a male *D. pumilio* rush at a *P. lugubris*, knock him over, push him and press him to the ground. Then the little red *D. pumilio* thrust his head under that of the *P. lugubris* and, with a hard shove, pushed him over, backwards into the water basin. Finally, he jumped on to the belly of his now helpless victim.

This should not, of course, be viewed as murder motivated by evil – the animals are simply following their instincts in order to continue as a species. They have to defend their territories if they are to survive. Unless they own territory they cannot breed. They need a certain amount of space in which to deposit their eggs and look after the highly evolved development of their young. Other frogs represent danger to the clutches of eggs or to the freshly emerged tadpoles, and this will not be tolerated by a zealous frog father. It is, therefore, worry for his offspring that drives him to chase any intruder from his territory.

However, things rarely turn out quite as tragically as in our story of the killer *D. pumilio*. Only in the confines of a terrarium, in which the weaker animals can no longer evade constant attacks, do disasters like this happen.

6
Survival Artists

Where survival is concerned, poison-arrow frogs are much more inventive than most other frogs. Their skin toxins generally protect them from being eaten and their motto is warning rather than camouflage. Usually their strategy is successful; only very few animals – large spiders, for example – will attack them.

Survival of the species depends also on reproduction. And here too the Dendrobatidae seem to be eminently successful, judging by their relative profusion within their habitats.

All present-day frog species – as with all other animal species – are the result of changes stretching over millions of years. One of the most important factors in this process is mutation, a spontaneous change in the chromosomes or genes. Such changes must have taken place quite often in the evolution of poison-arrow frogs. Look, for example, at one interesting detail of their anatomy – their fingertips. Poison-arrow frogs have flattened fingertips. This is unusual in a ground-based animal – it is a characteristic of the Hylidae, which 'stick' themselves to leaves by means of their flat, 'sucker' feet.

Because of this mutation poison-arrow frogs were able to live in bushes and on trees as well as on the ground. A whole new habitat was created for them, giving them a more varied range of food and new, hitherto unattainable, places to deposit their eggs. *D. quinquevittatus* has adapted completely to a life in trees, where it lives in water-filled bromeliads. This meant changes not only in lifestyle but in the biology of reproduction. In the new habitat there were no large aggregations of water. Poison-arrow frogs managed to adapt to these changed circumstances. They no longer lay their eggs in water but deposit them on land, in damp places under leaves. There the eggs develop, safely guarded by the frog father, until the tadpoles emerge. But what then? Young tadpoles require water for their further development. The solution is ingenious. The frog father squats in the remains of the gelatinous mass, right among the larvae.

These respond to the sensations of movement and wriggle up the father's legs on to his back. Then, with the larvae riding piggyback, the father sets off to look for a small body of water for his offspring. His search can take several days, while the tadpoles remain tightly curled and almost motionless on his back. Then, when he finally locates a suitable quantity of water, the father lowers his behind into it and shakes himself a little. This signals the tadpoles to abandon the paternal back and slide into the water. From now on they are in charge of their own lives.

This very caring behaviour also affects the number of eggs in a clutch. Most frogs produce voluminous clutches of from several hundred to 20,000 eggs and deposit them in water without any further care. A percentage of these egg clusters is usually eaten by other animals within the first few days. When the surviving tadpoles finally emerge, they are right in the midst of a daily battle for survival – *Dytiscus*, dragonfly larvae, newts, fish and small mammals reduce their numbers considerably. Because there are initially vast numbers of them, in the end some at least manage to transform into tiny frogs. Poison-arrow frogs achieve the same result with much smaller clutches of eggs. They manage with a maximum of 40 to 50 eggs per clutch, some species with only four to six. Because of the especial care they take of the young at least as many offspring attain adulthood as is necessary for the survival of the species.

7

The Unique Frog Parent

Frogs have a reputation for being uncaring parents – most species take no care of their offspring after they have deposited the eggs. The enormous number of eggs, however, ensures that at least a few progeny attain reproductive age. But, as we saw in the previous chapter, poison-arrow frogs are not like this and others, too, take care of their young. The females of the toad *Pipa* and of the tree frog *Gastrotheca* have evolved a passive form of care of the young to protect their clutches from external dangers. All embryonal and some larval development, up to the ready-to-emerge tadpole stage or the young-frog stage, take place in special breeding pouches situated in the skin of the females' backs. The male of Darwin's frog, the Chilean *Rhinoderma darwini*, takes care of the young. He first guards the clutch of eggs. When the tadpoles hatch he snaps them up and carries them around in a sac in his gullet until their metamorphosis, when he spits out the young frogs, only 5–10 mm (¼–⅜ in) long.

The poison-arrow frog's parental care usually ends when the father has deposited his offspring at a suitable body of water. However, we know now that strawberry poison-arrow frogs (*D. pumilio*) and a few closely related species take their care even further. Recent observations have made sensational discoveries about their behaviour.

Until a few years ago breeding strawberry poison-arrow frogs in terraria seemed to be fraught with insoluble problems. The frogs laid eggs and the embryos developed into freely swimming tadpoles, but the larvae stubbornly refused any food. Terrarium owners tried just about everything to get them to eat. They offered them flaked food, various algae, infusoria, *Artemia*, *Tubifex* worms and even dog food. The tadpoles reacted almost as if bored, refused to eat, and died.

Finally, one terrarium owner had a brainwave. Bechter (1978), in desperation, fed the tadpoles with the egg of another species of poison-arrow frog – and they gobbled it up. Then followed another brainwave – what about hen's eggs? If frog's eggs were welcome, perhaps raw egg yolk might work. And so it did. The larvae went mad when Bechter dropped the first speck of egg yolk into the water. Since then, it has been possible to breed strawberry poison-arrow frogs, a great triumph for dedicated terrarium owners.

But questions remained. What did these larvae live on in their natural habitat? Hardly off hens' eggs. Perhaps on frogs' eggs? But how could that work?

It was left to two other terrarium owners to find the answers to these questions. Graeff and Schulte (1980) were able to observe in *D. pumilio* a form of parental care hitherto unknown. In an experimental set-up they observed in a terrarium what happened to the spawned eggs of the strawberry poison-arrow frog. They noticed that the female picked up the freshly emerged tadpoles separately and placed them in the vases of bromeliads. That in itself was not remarkable. However, during the days that followed the female returned to the larvae-carrying bromeliads and dropped a few eggs into the water in their vases. It could only be that these unfertilized eggs were intended as food for the larvae. A frog that feeds its young! This was indeed a sensational discovery, showing what highly evolved forms of parental care such a tiny species of frog was capable of. From this breakthrough, other discoveries followed. According to the present stage of our knowledge, the larvae of *D. pumilio* and related species (*D. granuliferus*) and of *D. histrionicus* and related species (*D. lehmanni* and *D. speciosus*) are egg eaters that are provided by the mother with eggs especially produced for this purpose. In *D. quinquevittatus* and related species, too, the female normally provides the larvae with egg clutches for food. However, these larvae can survive without eating eggs, by feeding on plants, drowned insects and so on. So they represent a transitional phase towards the specialism of those larvae that eat only eggs produced by their own species.

8
Care in the Terrarium

Terrarium Basics

Now that we know something of the lifestyles of poison-arrow frogs, we can concentrate on the basics of keeping them in terraria. The most important thing is to create a terrarium that will offer the frogs a habitat very similar to their natural environment.

As poison-arrow frogs live in moist tropical regions, we need to furnish the terrarium with a moist, warm climate, so a tropical rain-forest terrarium would be the ideal home for them. But if you try to buy such a terrarium you will almost certainly fail. Specialist retailers, as a rule, do not stock terraria suitable for keeping frogs, because they are not in great demand.

In most cases, there will be nothing else for it but to build your own. This does have advantages – the terrarium will be inexpensive and personal preferences can be catered for – and, with a little skill, you should be able to build a terrarium that does not too obviously look a do-it-yourself job.

Experience has shown that moist-climate terraria made of silicon-sealed, aluminium-framed glass are best. I make the terraria I use for poison-arrow frogs in sizes between 60 × 60 × 40 cm (2 × 2 × 1⅓ ft) and 80 × 80 × 50 cm (2½ × 2½ × 1⅔ ft). To describe the construction technique I have taken for my example a terrarium of the smaller size.

First we shall need seven plates of glass about 0.6 mm (¼ in) thick cut to the following sizes (all the Imperial equivalents are approximate): the floor piece 58 × 39 cm (23 × 16 in); the back-wall piece 60 × 60 cm (2 × 2 ft); the two side pieces 60 × 39 cm (2 × 1⅓ ft); front piece (a) 58 × 8 cm (23 × 3 in); front piece (b) 51.5 × 60 cm (1⅔ × 2 ft); and the lid piece 60 × 25 cm (2 ft × 10 in). Further necessary items will be a cartridge of silicon glue-sealer (acetic-acid base) and a few aluminium sections to make a sliding front wall. These aluminium sections are obtainable from builders' merchants, usually in multiples of a metre. You will need: an L-section about 3 × 3 cm (1¼ × 1¼ in), 58.5 cm (23 in) long; a U-section as the sliding base for the front-wall glass, 58.5 cm (23 in); and an L-section, about 2 × 2 cm (¾ × ¾ in), as the top sliding frame for the front wall, 60 cm (24 in) long.

First, the base piece, the back wall, and the two side walls are glued together. Use a flat surface and cover it with newspaper, to avoid gluing the terrarium to the table top. The glass should be cleaned thoroughly and the edges rubbed down with acetone, to make sure they are free of grease, and dried. Place the base piece on the table, and stand the back-wall piece upright about 4 mm (⅛ in) behind it so that it overlaps the base plate right and left by about 1 cm (⅜ in). Position the two side plates at the ends, making sure that they also are placed 4 mm (⅛ in) away from the base plate. (If you have no one to help you hold these side glasses in position you will have to lean the back glass against something – push the table against a wall, for example – so that you can fit them in.

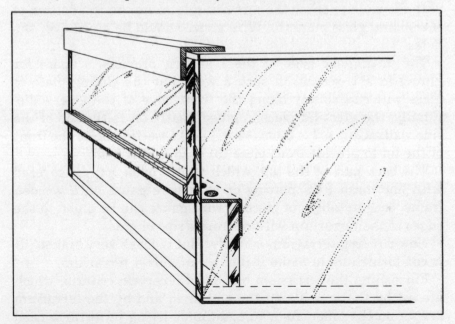

Diagrammatic view of the terrarium described in this chapter. The lower edge of the viewing plate is resting on the front plate, which in turn was set back by about 2 cm (¾ in). The metal L-shaped section has been glued in the angle of front plate and juts out in front of the side plates by about 1 cm (⅜ in).

Hold the glass plates in position with angle pieces or sticky tape (fixed to the outside, so that you get in the end a clean glued internal angle) and then, using a glue gun, squeeze ribbons of silicon into the gaps between the plates. The plastic nozzle of the gun should be cut off in such a way that the exuding ribbon completely fills the gaps from edge to edge. Use a finger moistened with washing-up liquid to smooth the edges of the silicon ribbon against the glass.

Now leave the whole thing for a day for the silicon glue to dry properly. Again clean the glued edges to remove all remaining washing-up liquid. Then glue the small front pane of glass (a) into the open front of the terrarium, so that it is set back 2 cm (¾in).

Wait several hours until the front piece (a) is firmly set. Position a 3 × 3 cm (1¼ × 1¼ in) L-section on top of the front plate (a) and glue it so that the wide arm of the L protrudes by 1 cm (⅜ in) from the side plates. You should beforehand have bored a number of holes, about 1 cm (⅜ in) in diameter, along this wide arm of the L-section. These are ventilation holes that will allow air to enter the terrarium later on via the bottom of the sliding glass plate (b). Wire gauze should be glued over the holes.

The jutting-out edge of the L-section provides a space for gluing in a U-section in such a way that the sliding plate of glass will run closely along the front edge of the side walls. Finally, the glass-lid piece is glued neatly on to the top of the side walls. Glue a 2 × 2 cm (¾ × ¾ in) L-section on to the front of the lid to provide front piece (b) with a firm hold.

The back part of the top, which is still open, can be covered with fine mesh PVC netting or with wire gauze on a wooden frame, or a suitably cut piece of wire gauze can be glued to the edges of the terrarium with narrow strips of glass.

Now our frog terrarium is ready. But it looks very 'naked'. It needs furnishing to make it into a rain-forest terrarium.

Furnishing the terrarium has to fulfil certain criteria, which are set by the animals on the one hand and by the terrarium keeper on the other. As a rule, animals living in terraria need distinct microclimatic areas. Poison-arrow frogs live in environments with an apparently even microclimate, but even they experience different conditions – a frog that climbs a tree trunk,

A tropical terrarium for poison-arrow frogs can be made to look like an attractive 'jungle behind glass'. Important elements are high humidity and a dense planting of bromeliads.

for example, will encounter a lower humidity higher up than on the floor of the forest or among plants. Again, where the sun penetrates dense jungle vegetation, these spots will be warmer than those in the shade and frogs will use them as sun baths.

A skilful arrangement in the terrarium can create different microclimates. A pump can create a small stream running through the terrarium, and the edges of it can be planted with dense vegetation to create cooler and moister areas than in the upper reaches, where a lamp or bulb might be installed.

The suggestions that follow for the interior of a rain-forest terrarium can, of course, be adapted according to personal preferences.

The floor basin of the terrarium is filled with water. The land area, taking up about three quarters of the base, is supplied with island-like clumps of cork-bark pieces and filled with clay globe planters. Low-growing plants will be sited in these wet areas. I prefer *Yucca*, bromeliads, *Scindapsus*, *Ficus*, and other long-lasting plants. A ground-covering layer of oak leaves will provide the right-looking environment.

The rear wall can be made attractive with pieces of cork-oak bark, or even with thin sheets of cork such as can be purchased at a builders' merchants and which can be glued to the glass backing with silicon. If the rough, gnarled bark of cork oak is used for the rear wall, small epiphytes, *Tillandsia* or ferns can be inserted in pockets. A climbing fig (*Ficus repens*) or other creepers can be allowed to grow up from the ground.

An epiphyte branch with attractive plants inserted along it can make a marvellous decoration for a rain-forest terrarium. The branch can be anchored firmly in the ground and made to bridge the stream, like a small-scale fallen jungle giant. An epiphyte allowed to hang freely is especially attractive in larger terraria. When choosing epiphytes it is advisable to stick to robust species of bromeliads like *Tillandsia* – a chat with a specialist at your garden centre may help to familiarize you with the range of plants on the market.

The basis for an epiphyte-carrying branch could be robinia branches or gutter-shaped pieces of cork oak. The epiphytes themselves can be tied on with nylon twine until they are rooted properly. Epiphytes should not be bedded, as they sometimes are, on a layer of plant matter (such as fern roots); Stettler (1978) points out that, since they absorb moisture from the air through their roots, this only hinders them.

Large bromeliads are essential in our terrarium, because many poison-arrow frogs enjoy spending time in their vases and prefer their wide, smooth leaves (for example, those of *Guzmania* species) for egg-laying.

A few more details, added to these basics, should create a pleasant home for our frogs and an attractive terrarium for us.

Further improvements aimed at creating optimum conditions in the terrarium can be achieved with a few pieces of technical apparatus. The main factors to consider are light, air (humidity and warmth), and water.

In a terrarium for poison-arrow frogs the moisture content of the air has to be high; the relative humidity should lie between

80 and 100 per cent. If we allow the water in the lower part of the terrarium to flow over a centrifugal pump with a filtering device, two advantages are gained. First, the water is cleaned and we need not change it every day. Second, it can be conducted back into the terrarium as a small waterfall, which will keep the air moist. Spraying the inside of the terrarium with a plant spray several times a day will then ensure that humidity rises to the desired levels. This can be checked with a hygrometer.

Light of a particular spectral range and intensity is of paramount importance for the animals and plants in a terrarium. Some animals will not reproduce if the intensity of the light falls below a certain level; others react to lack of light by becoming torpid and refusing to feed. The unit used to measure illumination, or light intensity, is the lux. In full sunlight up to 100,000 lux may be registered, in open shade still 10,000 lux, at the window inside a room 2,000 lux and 2 m (6 ft) away from a window only 300 lux. Poison-arrow frogs do not live in the brightest sunlight – they live in the jungle, and partly on the ground, where there is not nearly so much light. Measurements taken in the rain-forests of Panama showed that the crowns of tall trees were receiving only 25 per cent of the light outside, the crowns of smaller trees only 6 per cent, tree-trunk levels still 5 per cent, and the forest floor only 1 per cent (Geiger in Nietzke, 1984). Nonetheless, on the forest floor and at the levels of tree trunks, the habitat of poison-arrow frogs, the light is still more intense than it is in our living rooms. Without artificial light, therefore, indoor terraria will not be viable. The best sources of light for terraria are fluorescent tubes. They have a range of light similar to daylight, and while consuming a relatively small amount of current, they produce much light and little warmth.

Modern lighting technology has created a wide range of different types of lamp so that the right light is available for every purpose. For terraria fluorescent lights marketed by various manufacturers may safely be recommended. If you are making home-made light boxes you must incorporate reflectors so that the fluorescent tubes give off the greater percentage of their light downwards, or you could line the insides of the boxes with reflecting material such as aluminium foil.

You can buy purpose-manufactured lamps. True-Lite fluorescent tubes have been developed especially for terraria. They cover the full daylight spectrum, including the ultra-violet wave-lengths, but, because the ultra-violet portion is small, they can safely be used constantly (for 10 to 14 hours) in terraria containing frogs.

Opinions differ on the need for using these tubes, which are quite expensive. While Schulte (1980) considers them to be indispensable and useful, I know many terrarium keepers who do not use them and yet have beautiful animals with healthy offspring. The absence of ultra-violet light, which among other things stimulates production of vitamin D and so prevents such diseases as rickets, can be compensated for by feeding the animals vitamins and calcium (which should be done anyway).

If you use True-Lite tubes choose the twisted models (Power-Twist), which put out more light. And do not install them above the glass top of the terrarium – ultra-violet light cannot penetrate glass. E. Zimmermann (1983) records good results with solarium lamps in the care of *Hyperolius*, but these creatures often sit in direct sunlight in the wild. Poison-arrow frogs, in my opinion, do not need such intense ultra-violet radiation.

The time that the lights should be kept on should correspond to the length of daylight time in the equatorial regions that are home to poison-arrow frogs – that is 12 to 14 hours.

A temperature of 24° to 30°C is produced by the lighting in my terraria. Fluorescent tubes are very good for heating. But should a sufficient temperature of at least 23°C not be attained, the terrarium may be warmed by a heating cable or heating mat. Heating cables are installed in the terrarium, for example in the floor or behind the back wall, while heating mats are laid beneath it. Both are best used linked with a thermostat to adjust to the desired temperature and maintain it.

Breeding Insects for Food

Before introducing frogs to our finished rain-forest terrarium, we have to solve the question of diet. In the wild poison-arrow frogs live on all kinds of small insects. It would be well-nigh impossible to offer them their accustomed tropical insect fare in a terrarium. Fortunately, they are satisfied with other types of insect, as long as the size and taste are to their liking.

'Meadow plankton', made up of all kinds of insects, can be successfully netted in summer and, apart from some indigestible beetles, will be gratefully accepted by the frogs. In winter, though, such meadow harvests are not available, and a hunt for insects in the cellar will tend to be exhausting rather than productive. This is when the value of breeding insects as food will become apparent – bred insects are not dependent upon the seasons. Breeding insects as food is not as difficult as it might perhaps sound. At any rate, the standard fare of poison-arrow frogs, the fruit fly (*Drosophila*), is easy to breed in large quantities.

Fruit flies come in more than one shape and size. There is the winged, flying variety for skilled breeders and the stumpy-winged non-flying variety for the less experienced. I have been breeding two sorts of non-flying *Drosophila* for years – the small, stumpy-winged *Drosophila funebris* and the large *Drosophila hydei*. Anyone deciding to breed the flying type indoors should, though, have a relaxed attitude and not get excited when the fruit flies begin to multiply on fruit stocks as well as in the jars intended for this purpose. As the flying *Drosophila* can 'persuade' their non-flying relatives to fly, once they have broken into a culture (the flying type possesses the dominant gene), a breeding area meant for non-flying *Drosophila* should be declared out of bounds for the flying type.

There are many recipes for a nutritional gruel on which to rear *Drosophila*. A gruel can be prepared quite easily from the fruit varieties of babyfood or by starting simply with apple sauce. Put a portion of stewed fruit (banana and apple) or apple sauce in a 1 l (1 qt) fruit-bottling jar, add 10 ml (1 dessertspoon) brewer's yeast and sugar, and stir in porridge oats until the mixture is no longer watery. To prevent mould from forming, sprinkle a pinch of mould inhibitor evenly over the surface of the gruel. Cover the still-sticky surface with a layer of absorbent toilet paper and, finally, drop a handful of wood shavings into the jar for the flies to climb on.

Another inexpensive recipe for *Drosophila* gruel takes dog-food flakes and porridge oats mixed in equal quantitites and moistened with white wine (no particular variety is required) until sticky. A little mould inhibitor added to the surface completes the gruel.

The stumpy-winged *Drosophila* develops from egg to adult fly in about 14 days at a temperature of 20° to 25° C. The large fruit fly, which is recommended as food for the larger poison-arrow frogs, has a development cycle of four weeks. The beauty of breeding fruit flies is that there is no need to bother about them or give them any care during their entire breeding cycle – all you have to do is see that the gruel does not dry out.

The *Drosophila* should be 'vitaminized' before they are fed to the frogs. My own method is to use a paper funnel to shake my non-flying *Drosophila* into a plastic tube into which I have previously shaken a little vitamin-calcium mixture. Shake the flies around a few times until they are thoroughly dusted. Poison-arrow frogs seem to prefer these flies to untreated ones.

Other insects suitable for frog food are field crickets (*Gryllus bimaculatus*) and house crickets (*Acheta domesticus*). I breed these in 5 l (1 gal) plastic buckets with gauze inserts in their lids. I cover the bottom of the bucket with a 10 cm (4 in) layer of fine sand for the *Gryllus* and of peat for the *Acheta*. Cardboard egg cartons stacked one upon another provide hiding places and climbing facilities for the insects. A small, 5 cm (2 in) deep plastic dish filled with sand is placed at the bottom of the bucket for the female crickets to lay their eggs in. In nature crickets lay eggs in a damp substratum, so the sand should be kept constantly moist. Temperature should be held at around 30°C. Development from egg to fully grown cricket takes about ten weeks. Food for the insects could be, for example, fruit, especially apple pieces, oats, dry fish food, and (unsprayed) lettuce. Only freshly hatched crickets should be given to the frogs; mature adults are unsuitable, so only a few crickets should be allowed to grow up for further breeding.

One problem in breeding *Acheta* should be mentioned – they are much more likely to break out of the breeding container than *Gryllus* and once they have escaped into your living area they can become a constant nuisance. Because of this, and also because of the persistent chirping noises made by the adult insects, it is advisable to keep them in the cellar or some other suitably distanced room.

Another easy-to-breed food insect is the Indian meal moth (*Plodia interpunctella*), which can be bred in the same way in plastic buckets at a temperature of around 25°C. Experience has shown that a nourishing gruel made of dog-food flakes moistened with glycerine is ideal for these moths. A layer of gruel 5–10 cm (2–4 in) deep is put in the bucket and a few moths added. After about eight weeks you will be able to remove quantities of small caterpillars and moths from the lid of the bucket.

Breeding the larger wax moth (*Galleria mellonella*) and the lesser wax moth (*Achroea grisella*) is also quite simple. Line the inside of the plastic bucket with corrugated cardboard, for the chrysalis stage of the caterpillars. The breeding process is quickest at a constant temperature of 28° to 39°C. The best food is old honeycombs, which may be got from a beekeeper or from a honey retailer, but if these are not obtainable an artificial substitute can be made. The ingredients are 500 g (1 lb) runny honey, 500 g (1 lb) glycerine (from a chemist), 100 g (4 oz) brewer's yeast, 200 g (8 oz) bran, 200 g (8 oz) skimmed milk, 200 g (8 oz) wheat or soy flour and 400 g (12 oz) maize meal or semolina. The honey and glycerine are mixed thoroughly together. The other ingredients are first mixed well and then added gradually to the honey-glycerine mixture which is stirred and kneaded until it turns into a sticky dough smelling of beeswax. Allow two or three days for it to harden before feeding it to the moths. It can be cut into slices or cubes quite easily and stored in a fridge for several months (recipe after Friederich and Volland, 1981). Seven to eight weeks from starting the breeding colony should be flourishing. The caterpillars especially are a delicacy for the frogs.

If you are using several breeding vessels, it is a good idea to keep them all in a special cupboard. An old cupboard can be adapted for use as a breeding space by gluing Styrofoam sheets to the inside and heating it with a light bulb. A few airholes can be drilled into it for ventilation. The cricket-breeding containers should be placed near the light bulb, as crickets thrive in constant light and warmth. Wax moths will be happier in darker areas beneath the shelves.

Friendly terrarium owners may have their own tips on breeding to offer. Information can be obtained from producers of insect breeders for petfood (there are always advertisements in specialist magazines for aquarium and terrarium keepers). Or, if there is a club in your area, it will be well worth joining for hints and advice.

Infection and Disease

Disease is an unpleasant subject, but one that has to be tackled – poison-arrow frogs can be subject to diseases that can become epidemic and wipe out entire terrarium colonies.

Because of the contagious character of these frog diseases, newly acquired frogs should be quarantined for a period of three months. This is especially important for imported animals purchased through the trade, because, at a conservative estimate, 50 per cent of these are infected. Happily, there has recently been an improvement in this state of affairs, because dubious exporters are increasingly being shunned by responsible retailers. However, it is too soon to give the 'all clear'.

The frogs should be quarantined in a standard, fully equipped terrarium, because they need the best possible living conditions from the start. They must be watched carefully during their quarantine period for any early signs of disease. Their skins should look shiny and be free of injuries – even very small skin wounds can be dangerous. Their faeces should be of firm consistency and brownish-red in colour. Traces of blood in the excreta may indicate inner lesions and point to an intestinal infection. In its early stages an intestinal infection can be cured successfully by administering sulphonamide powder orally – you dust the food insects with the powder. If the frogs eat but become thinner and white dots appear in the faeces, get a parasitologist to examine the faeces for worms. Worming orally is hardly possible, given the small size of most poison-arrow frogs, so a bath in a vermicidal solution is the answer.

Hygiene is top priority, and not only for sick animals. At least during acclimatization, the frogs' bath water should be changed daily in order to prevent re-infection. Faeces must be removed regularly, and if disease does take hold it can be sensible to set up a relatively sterile 'hospital' terrarium, with a foam mat rather than natural flooring and only a few plants.

The most common of the contagious diseases you are likely to meet is scratching disease. Affected frogs scratch their backs and flanks at irregular intervals – they usually wipe their back legs across their backs and flanks as if trying to scrape something off. The symptoms become more pronounced the more humid the air is – for example, the scratching movements may become more intense after the terrarium has been sprayed. At first the frogs continue to eat normally and there is nothing apart from the scratching to indicate that they are ill. Not until the final stages of the disease, which lasts over a period of three to ten weeks, do they show other symptoms such as staggering movements and sudden, uncontrolled leaps. At this point they stop eating, lose weight, and die within a few days.

There is still no known effective cure for scratching disease. Up until now it has always proved fatal. Bathing the frogs in water containing different types of anti-bacterial substances from aquarium medicine has proved a failure. Orally administered antibiotics seem to promise some success, but most of this work is still in an experimental phase.

I had the first encouraging sign that a cure might be found for scratching disease when I was treating some strawberry poison-arrow frogs. Some specimens that had been captured in the wild began to display symptoms of the disease shortly after I received them. Fortunately I had isolated them in a quarantine terrarium. While I was trying to think of ways of treating them, it occurred to me that I had just had antibiotic drops prescribed for an ear infection. Perhaps something that helped me with itchy ears would work with scratching disease. Using a pipette, I allowed a drop of the liquid (trade-named Panotile) to fall on to the backs of my sick frogs. Then I sprayed them with water from a plant spray to try to distribute the medicine a little. Startled leaps by the frogs seemed to indicate that the medicine must feel unpleasant. However, they calmed down after a short time. I continued this procedure twice more at intervals of two days. To my great surprise, eight out of the ten frogs recovered and began to eat again. So perhaps Panotile ear drops may prove to be an effective medicine against scratching disease. I am optimistic!

Another contagious disease is bone rot. Infected frogs first manifest small, circular lesions on their skin. The small holes rapidly grow larger and eat into the surrounding tissue, right down to the bone, which, in the final stages, is also destroyed. In its early stages bone rot appears to respond to sulphonamide preparations. At any rate, I have had some success in treating *Mantella aurantiaca*. I found that one of these little frogs had developed a number of small holes in its skin. Immediately I isolated it from the others in a small treatment terrarium. Daily I sprinkled sulphonamide powder on the afflicted areas of its skin. I also gave it sulphonamide orally, by dusting its food insects (*Drosophila*) with it. The *M. auriantica* left in the large terrarium were also fed sulphonamide powder daily with their rations. I carried out this treatment over a period of ten days. Success was shown by the fact that the isolated frog's skin lesions healed up and no signs of illness appeared in the other frogs.

I would strongly advise the beginner to purchase later generations of poison-arrow frogs. As a rule there are no health problems with these. Sick frogs and epidemics can be a cause of grief to even the experienced terrarium owner, and sometimes spoil his hobby.

Apart from diseases, there are some developmental problems that are common in poison-arrow frogs. Great numbers of larvae bred in terraria fall victim to a developmental disorder known as spindly legs syndrome. This occurs should a tadpole's front leg be broken in two shortly before the end of metamorphosis. The leg then appears as a totally undeveloped, non-functioning spindly leg. These crippled front legs often remain under the skin, so that the young frog has to try and reach land without front legs. It will usually survive for only a few days.

Some years ago this problem was particularly common among later generations of my *Phyllobates tricolor*. At first I thought that something was wrong with the breeding conditions of the larvae. However, my experiments (Heselhaus, 1983) indicated that these spindly legs were not the result of inadequate food supplies or of unsuitable breeding methods. Although this supposition has on the whole been confirmed, the problem seems to be a lot more complicated than I assumed initially. Based on the latest experiences this problem of spindly legs needs some revision and supplementary observations.

Other authors previously held the theory that spindly legs should be viewed as the effect of an inadequate food supply in the larvae stage. However, this seems applicable only to the few species of poison-arrow frogs whose larvae are definitely specialized with respect to their food supply, for example, the strawberry poison-arrow frog (*D. pumilio*). According to my experiences spindly legs appear frequently if the larvae are fed with egg yolk. Matthias Schmidt (1985) also reports that feeding with egg yolk is a cause of later deformation. In both cases the parents were frogs caught in the wild who bred successfully in a terrarium when the larvae were fed with eggs laid by the mother. It seemed, therefore, that the use of egg yolk as nourishment was unnatural and inadequate and the cause of deformations of the front legs.

In the case of less specialized species, spindly legs occasionally appear if the keeper tries to breed larvae in completely inadequate conditions. A cause for such deformations can be, for example, water that is too cool (15°C). My experiments with larvae of *D. quinquevittatus* showed that spindly legs could be produced artificially under such conditions. However, not all the larvae kept in these conditions developed spindly legs at the end of metamorphosis. In the control group, from the same parents, kept under normal conditions, there were no spindly legs.

From these experiments we can conclude that spindly legs can in certain cases be produced artificially by feeding the larvae egg yolk or by using water that is too cool. However, this does not explain the larvae that do not develop functioning front legs even though they are reared under excellent conditions. These larvae carry within them from the start a tendency for later deformations, so that the cause for spindly legs must be sought in the parents. This would indicate that fertility of the parents, their genetic mass, their physical state, and their age could be significant. As an important indicator for the theory that this deformation is a genetic factor, I can cite the observation that disorders appear during the embryonal development phase. I cited this atypical embryonal development (1983) as yolk-sac swelling. By about the third day of development germinated larvae show a greatly swollen, transparent yolk sac, which bursts a few days later. Clutches in which this yolk-sac swelling appears are totally unviable – without exception those few larvae that reach metamorphosis manifest spindly legs.

In species specialized in their larval feeding habits, spindly legs will appear especially in the offspring of one set of parents which are then crossed with each other over several generations. In some species the predisposition for deformations of the front legs can be discerned visually. While the wild specimen of *P. tricolor* has a pyjama-like colouring of wide red and white stripes, later generations can be brown and have only narrow, light stripes. *P. tricolor* is known as the 'guppy' among poison-arrow frogs, a fact which favours uncontrolled breeding. Likewise, one can no longer expect great things of breeds of *D. auratus* whose spines are deformed. In the case of such badly selected breeding pairs spindly legs are practically pre-programmed.

In my experience, it is very often the parents who are to blame if the offspring manifest deformed front legs. It is time, therefore, that simple enthusiasm over the possibility of breeding poison-arrow frogs should give way to a realistic evaluation of the circumstances. When breeding fish in aquaria it goes without saying that deformed and colourless individuals are excluded from further breeding and the same principle should apply to breeding poison-arrow frogs in terraria. Only when we are prepared, as serious terrarium keepers, to abandon high-pressure breeding in order to attain quality instead of quantity will we assure a high standard of poison-arrow frog breeding in the future. Especial care should be given to a varied diet for the parents and to a careful selection of breeding animals.

9
Successful Breeding in Captivity

I believe that the main aim of terrarium owners should be to breed new generations of frogs. The many successes we have had in breeding poison-arrow frogs show how absurd is the accusation that terrarium keepers are robbing nature.

The successful breeding of poison-arrow frogs is not an esoteric mystery but the result of proper care with the aim of encouraging the frogs to reproduce. Hopefully, the terrarium keeper can transform his enjoyment of these frogs into a gradually increasing knowledge of them, which can in turn lead him through a specialized knowledge of the species to the basics of the biology of reproduction. The more we know about our animals, the easier it will become to breed them successfully. Much of our present knowledge about poison-arrow frogs is thanks to committed terrarium keepers. Unending patience, explorative drive, and a thirst for knowledge led to breeding successes with frogs that had once been thought unbreedable.

The first successful breeding of strawberry poison-arrow frogs (*D. pumilio*) was due to Bechter (1978), who discovered why the care of strawberry poison-arrow larvae so often ended in failure. He found that the tadpoles are specialized in their food requirements, but that they could be fed with a substitute consisting of chicken-egg yolk. All other attempts at feeding them had failed until then – the tadpoles had starved rather than accept the usual types of food. Today we know that poison-arrow frogs receive a unique form of parental care – the female deposits its offspring in the leafy funnels of bromeliads and feeds them with eggs especially produced by her for this purpose.

These problems have been solved, although others have arisen – the problem of spindly legs, for example. But in spite of this, we can with some justification maintain that the greater part of the demand for poison-arrow frogs can be met with offspring bred in captivity.

I give here some tips for the breeding of poison-arrow frogs which have proved useful in practice for me and other terrarium owners of my acquaintance. It goes without saying that long-term breeding is only possible with frogs that are in the best possible condition. For this reason one of our main concerns has been to ensure a varied diet rich in vitamins and minerals. The terrarium should be furnished to suit the requirements and preferences of the species that it is proposed to breed. Should, for example, the frogs be of a species that deposits its eggs in bromeliad vases high above the ground, this fact will have to be taken into account when furnishing the terrarium with plants. Other species require a fast-flowing stream, which can be imitated with the help of a filter pump. The temperature and humidity in the terrarium should be adjusted in such a way as to closely approximate the climate of the frogs' natural habitat, not forgetting that some species of poison-arrow frogs come from regions that have more or less pronounced dry periods. These variations in climatic conditions are very important for some species – they serve as a catalyst for reproduction. As a rule, poison-arrow frogs can be put in the mood for breeding if we keep them in high humidity with daily rain showers.

When the frogs finally lay their eggs it is helpful to know about the sequence of care of the young and the various possibilities of the larval process. Care of the young for *Phyllobates* and most *Dendrobates* species ends with depositing the larvae in a suitable small pool of water. In these non-specialized species it is best to remove the fertilized clutches in order to raise the larvae artificially. As a rule, the larvae are not choosy about feeding and can be cared for easily. If there are large numbers of tadpoles they can be kept together in a 50 l (10 gal) aquarium from the age of about four weeks onwards. The tank should be equipped with many water plants and an inner filter. Plenty of space and dense vegetation are needed so that the larvae can hide from each other as they have a tendency to become cannibals. Specialized species, which naturally live on food eggs from their own species, are best left to grow up in solitary confinement. These species – *D. quinquevittatus* and related species and *D. histrionicus* and *D. pumilio* and related species – excrete growth-inhibiting substances that seem to have a mutually negative effect on other species kept in a common container. The same seems to apply to larvae from the same clutch if they are kept together. For example, I had problems with later generations of the striped *D. quinquevittatus* from French Guiana, which I tried to raise together in a spawning container for ornamental fish in a 50 l (10 gal) aquarium. In addition to marked growth disorders, which in the case of some larvae led to total cessation of growth, a large number of these larvae manifested spindly legs at the time of metamorphosis. After I separated the larvae of the subsequent broods of the same parents, this problem no longer appeared. I had not altered the breeding conditions (food and water) in any way.

Whereas the species of the *D. quinquevittatus* group can be fed quite simply with flaked food and defrosted red-gnat larvae, the artificial feeding of highly specialized species (*D. pumilio*, *D. histrionicus*) is very involved. The larvae of these species, as food specialists, eat only their own species' food eggs; they accept very little substitute food. According to Beutelschiess (1983), *D. speciosus* accepts low-fat cottage cheese as well as egg yolk. Feeding with these substitute foods is, however, very time-consuming, as the water in the aquarium has to be changed two hours after each feeding. On top of that, larvae fed with egg yolk grow very slowly, so that four or five months can pass until metamorphosis.

We should not interfere with the natural reproduction process. In suitable terraria, furnished with several bromeliads, strawberry poison-arrow frogs, for example, will be in the mood for reproduction all year round. If we simply leave them alone we shall be able to enjoy the appearance of young frogs again and again.

10

The Genus *Dendrobates*

Dendrobates auratus (Plates 1, 60, 61)

Description The *auratus* is one of the species of *Dendrobates* richest in varieties. In size and colouring as well as in habits there are great differences. It is between 2.5 cm (1 in) and 6 cm (2⅜ in) long, according to its region of origin. Already over 15 colour forms of the species are known.

The home of one variety is the Pacific island of Taboga, belonging to Panama. These frogs, which are about 3 cm (1⅛ in) to 4 cm (1½ in) long, have yellow-gold stripes on a brown background. Many have a lighter brown background that emphasizes the golden effect even more. Partly because of the dry periods characteristic of the natural environment of these frogs, they are very robust and undemanding.

Among the most beautiful and most commonly imported of *D. auratus* are those from Costa Rica and western Panama. They glow in green and black, with bands of green irregularly distributed over the basic colour of varnished black – the proportion of green depending upon which population the variety comes from. The size of these very shy frogs varies according to the region of origin, but they are between 4 cm (1½ in) and 6 cm (2⅜ in) long.

The smallest variety of *D. auratus*, 2.5 cm (1 in) long, lives in the Panama Canal zone. These frogs, also known as *Colonauratus*, have the same green-black colour scheme, but they display only a few small green spots on a black background. They are very active, quick frogs, which are rather shy. From the Pacific side of Panama frogs with blue markings have only recently become known. These attractively coloured frogs are basically black, with intense blue markings ranging from light blue to almost violet. Within this population are also the exceedingly rare uniformly blue frogs. This quiet and amiable frog is among the larger of the *D. auratus* frogs – it reaches a good 4 cm (1½ in).

Many other varieties of *D. auratus* exist – there are albino forms and brown, white, or yellow striped, dotted or single-coloured specimens. The range of different forms is so large that they cannot all be discussed here.

Distribution and habitat *D. auratus* inhabits large regions of Central and South America and is to be found from southern Nicaragua to Costa Rica, from Panama to Colombia. In addition, numbers have been introduced to the Hawaiian island of Oahu.

As a rule *D. auratus* inhabits the dryer regions of primary forests. The frogs live in pairs or in small groups on the ground, near large trees. Their habitat always includes a layer of dry large leaves on the jungle floor. They live at sea level as well as at around 800 m (2,600 ft).

If their habitat has already been cultivated, they prefer to live in cocoa plantations, where the fallen cocoa-plant leaves on the ground supply ideal places for hiding and depositing eggs. Moreover, around the time of the cocoa harvest, the rotting fruit attracts large numbers of insects, which form an excellent, easily caught diet for the frogs.

In large areas, especially of Panama, the habitats of *D. auratus* have been completely destroyed. Very often it is only narrow strips of vegetation along river courses that enable a few varieties to survive. The blue *D. auratus* is one of the colour forms living in such an area. The homes of these frogs lie like oases in the midst of dried-up landscapes and it can only be a matter of time before the last of these frogs has disappeared.

Care in the terrarium All varieties of *D. auratus* are easy to keep and breed in captivity. The size of the terrarium depends of course, on the number of frogs you intend to keep – remembering that it is possible to keep *D. auratus* in company with other poison-arrow frogs in a community terrarium. As *D. auratus* lives mainly in two dimensions, scarcely climbing at all, a terrarium has to be chosen with as large a floor area as possible. Two to five animals should form a breeding group. The terrarium will most closely approximate to their natural habitat if the floor is completely covered with oak leaves. The only plant needed is *Anthurium christallinum*, whose attractive leaves and luxurious root system afford an interesting spectacle after only a short time. If you want to mix these *D. auratus* with other frogs, their needs will also have to be catered for. A tank measuring 90 cm (3 ft) in length, 60 cm (2 ft) in width, and 90 cm (3 ft) in height is suitable for four *D. auratus*, four *P. lugubris*, and five to ten *D. pumilio*, which all live together even in the wild.

Given temperatures of 20° to 28°C and high humidity, *D. auratus* will have offspring very soon. The frogs will use halved coconut shells as well as the leaf layer. The egg clutches contain six to eight eggs. As not all parents look after their young, the clutches should be tended artificially – caring for the larvae is no problem.

Dendrobates azureus   Blue poison-arrow frog   (Plates 2, 7)

Description *D. azureus* is a rare species with a small, limited area of distribution. Do not try to keep this species in a terrarium unless you are sufficiently experienced to breed it successfully.

The blue poison-arrow frog, with a size of 38 mm (1½ in) to 45 mm (1¾ in), is among the larger species. It has an attractive appearance, with a glowing blue net or dot pattern on a black base. Some specimens are mainly blue. As in *D. tinctorius*, which can be crossed with this species, the fingertips of the males are flattened.

Distribution and habitat *D. azureus* inhabits the Sipaliwini savannah in Surinam at levels between 300 m (1,000 ft) and 400 m (1,300 ft). They are known nowhere else. Here they are to be found in small remnants of jungle in the savannah. They live on the ground, beside small streams flowing through the jungle islands. Temperatures are between 20°C at night and 27°C in the daytime.

Care in the terrarium *D. azureus* has been bred successfully with increasing frequency and so, thanks to committed terrarium keepers, a considerable stock of terrarium specimens has been derived from a few imported animals. Reports of successful breeding can be read, for example, in Kneller (1982b).

These glorious blue poison-arrow frogs show no shyness in the terrarium, so their mating behaviour can be observed quite easily. As a rule the female is the more active during mating. A female willing to mate will nudge the male in the side and stimulate him by stroking his back with her front legs. The male seems to find this impossible to resist and the two frogs finally disappear into their chosen spawning chamber. Usually it will not be long before the clutch of four to six eggs is deposited. The entire mating procedure is carried out very quietly – *D. azureus* males are no vocal artists. Their occasional subdued croakings, no more than a quiet buzzing, can hardly be heard outside the terrarium. The development of the clutch up to emergence of the larvae will take about 18 days at water temperatures around 22°C. The best container to use is a Petri dish. A drop of fungicide should be added to the water, which should be so shallow that the clutch is not completely covered.

The larvae should be raised in solitary confinement because of their aggressive behaviour. They will reach metamorphosis after 10 to 12 weeks if fed with flaked food and gnat larvae, and will turn into young frogs about 18 mm (¾ in) long.

Dendrobates fantasticus (Plate 3)

Description The most remarkable feature of *D. fantasticus* is its red head, which clearly stands out from the lacquered black of its back and extremities. For this reason the name I have suggested for the species, the red-headed tree frog, is probably quite appropriate.

On its red head it has an irregularly shaped black mark, a kind of crown. The shiny black of its back and belly is broken by cream-white stripes. Young animals do not show the marked contrasts between red and black of the adult – they have red patterns on their backs to begin with, which they lose during the first few weeks of their lives.

Distribution and habitat According to Kneller (1982a, 1983), *D. fantasticus* lives in the forests of the eastern mountain ranges of the Peruvian Andes, in the province of San Martín. It inhabits by preference shady primary forests at heights of 500 m (1,600 ft) to 800 m (2,600 ft). Kneller was able to observe it in its natural habitat. According to his observations, the frogs are purely tree dwellers, as they were to be found always at least 1.4 m (4 ft 6 in) above ground level on different tree trunks. Kneller also observed a few specimens on high leaves, where they appeared together with *D. imitator* (which Kneller described at the time as *D. reticulatus*).

Care in the terrarium A terrarium housing the tree-dwelling *D. fantasticus* should be of generous dimensions, especially in height, which should be over 80 cm (32 in). Temperature should be held between 20° and 27°C and humidity kept high. The frogs will make use of a few bromeliads in the upper part of the terrarium. The back wall may be allowed to become overgrown with *Ficus* or climbing philodendra – the frogs remain very shy unless they are given dense plants to hide in. They are extremely quick, so care has to be taken when handling objects in the terrarium. Food should consist of *Drosophila*, young house crickets, and other small insects.

By simulating rain showers we can get the males into the mood for reproduction. They react to heightened humidity with quiet mating calls. Females willing to mate can be recognized by their rotund bodies. They approach the calling male and are led by him, displaying jerky movements, to a suitable spawning place. The mating behaviour is similar to that of other species of the *D. quinquevittatus* group.

The egg clutches deposited in the leafy vases of bromeliads contain only three to four eggs. After the larvae have emerged the male will carry them one by one to a water-filled vase and deposit them there. In the wild the larvae are presumably fed with food eggs by the parents, as happens with other species of the *D. quinquevittatus* group. Because of the shy behaviour of my red-headed tree frogs, I have never yet seen anything along these lines in the terrarium. But as the larvae are not food specialists, they can be fed with all kinds of other things, such as gnat larvae or flake food. The front legs erupt in the larvae, now about 3 cm (1⅛ in), after 12 to 14 weeks. Because they are very aggressive the larvae should be raised separately. The young frogs will be 10 mm (⅜ in) to 12 mm (½ in) long.

Dendrobates granuliferus (Plate 8)

Description *D. granuliferus* is a small poison-arrow frog about 20 mm (¾ in) to 22 mm (⅞ in) long. These frogs are a glorious colour – the granulated skin is a glowing red to orange on the back, while belly, flanks, back legs, and the tiny feet shine out in turquoise-green to blue.

Distribution and habitat *D. granuliferus* lives in damp low-lying land areas along the Pacific coast of Costa Rica. In the wild its food consists of tiny insects and ants, which it reaches by climbing tree trunks.

Care in the terrarium *D. granuliferus* is often offered for sale on the market – perhaps too often, because the frogs marketed are imported, taken from the already far too restricted habitat of this species. Breeding from these attractive frogs is difficult and only rarely successful. The larvae, just like those of the *D. histrionicus* and *D. pumilio* groups, are specialized food-egg eaters and when artificially bred have to be fed with egg yolk. Once they are acclimatized they will last without problems for years in a terrarium. Unfortunately, sick animals are often offered for sale and as a result *D. granuliferus* seems to be the main carrier of scratching disease.

In a terrarium the frogs require a temperature of 22° to 26°C and high humidity. As they like to climb, the terrarium should be well stocked with plants, especially in the upper part. They can manage only the smallest insects as food.

Dendrobates histrionicus (Plates 4, 17)

Description *D. histrionicus* displays a range of different colours. There are chocolate-brown and beige frogs with red, yellow, white, or green dots, bands, or splashes and others with a yellow reticulated pattern on a basic red-brown colour. *D. histrionicus* is a medium-sized frog, up to 38 mm (1½ in).

Distribution and habitat *D. histrionicus* lives in the Chocó region in west Colombia and north-west Ecuador. They colonize tropical lowlands as well as mountainous rain-forests up to a height of

1,000 m (3,300 ft). Their habitat is the shady forest floor, where they live in the lowest vegetation levels.

Care in the terrarium Unfortunately the successful breeding of *D. histrionicus* offspring is still rare. Zimmermann (1980), though, did succeed in breeding these beautiful coloured frogs. The conditions were: humidity between 60 per cent and 100 per cent, a temperature of 18°C at night and 26°C in the daytime, and natural light (morning sunlight) through an east-facing window together with artificial light.

I have on a number of occasions found clutches of four to nine fertilized eggs on bromeliad leaves. But many of these clutches grew mould and the tadpoles that managed to emerge suffered from spindly legs. These failures may be traced to feeding with egg yolk – it may be that my local eggs are unsuitable.

Dendrobates imitator (Plates 5, 56)

Description *D. imitator* can reach lengths of up to about 20 mm (¾ in). It is an attractive little frog, its back yellow through to orange and covered with large black circles and ovals. Its yellow throat is dotted with black and the extremities and belly silvergrey to greenish patterned with finer black dots.

D. imitator has two separate black dots on the tip of its nose, which is a sure way of distinguishing it from the very similar 'one-dot' *D. quinquevittatus*. Schulte (1986), who first described the species, points out another mark that distinguishes it from *D. quinquevittatus* – its first toe is well developed, while *D. quinquevittatus* has a toe reduced to a small stump. There seem to be no further external differences between these two species. They differ greatly, though, in their behaviour.

Distribution and habitat *D. imitator* seems to live only in the northeastern parts of Peru, in the Cordillera Oriental. This habitat has already been described above for the species *D. fantasticus* and *D. reticulatus* which inhabit the same area.

Care in the terrarium This little tree frog is an interesting and lovable little frog when kept in a terrarium. Because in its natural habitat it lives among tall undergrowth and trees with epiphytes growing on them, it should be kept in a tall terrarium – at least 60 cm (2 ft) high and 60 cm (2 ft) wide and 40 cm (16 in) long. It will be comfortable at an air temperature between 22° and 28°C and with humidity as high as possible. The terrarium can be furnished with dense clumps of *philodendra*, bromeliads, and creepers such as *Scindapsus*, so that this climbing artist among the tree frogs will find a 'jungle' with a mass of interwoven leaves and air roots. By creating extra rain showers with an ordinary garden spray it is possible to stimulate the *D. imitator* to mate. The males react to raised humidity levels with quite loud 'prrr-prrr-prrr' calls, rather like the chirping of a cricket. Artificial rain showers set these calls going fairly consistently, so it does not seem to be the sight of a female that causes the male to call out, although, according to Bechter and Lescure (1983), this is the trigger that starts off the striped *D. quinquevittatus* of French Guiana.

Females willing to spawn – recognizable by their increased girth – will turn to a calling male, who will then make another supreme effort and trill until his whole body is shaking to and fro. The female, impressed by this performance, will approach him and he will emerge from the dense plant growth to lead her to a spawning place.

Unlike *D. quinquevittatus*, these frogs will never or seldom spawn in the leaf axils of bromeliads. Their preferred spawning places are the undersides of smooth leaves, which they like to be hanging as nearly vertically as possible. They will often even spawn on the walls of the terrarium, provided they are warm and in the shadow of leaves. Just before spawning they hold on to the smooth spawning place in almost acrobatic poses – their climbing abilities and the adhesive nature of their broad toe pads make them unique among the tree-climbing frogs. They are quite able to jump up wet, vertical terrarium glass walls.

Before spawning the frogs sit closely beside one another, head to head. There is no clasping. The female deposits her clutch of two to five large eggs in a very sticky, composite gel. She presses the eggs against the surface of the chosen spot with her body – they are sticky enough to adhere immediately. Then she goes away – the male will stay behind and fertilize the eggs.

The male stays near the eggs and moistens them occasionally. The tadpoles emerge after 10 to 14 days. They are quite large compared with freshly emerged larvae of other small poison-arrow frogs, about 10 mm (⅜ in) long. The father carries them one by one to a suitable body of water. It may take a few days before he finds a suitable leafy vase.

During this period he may already be courting another female. Carrying a larva on his back does not prevent him from continuing to look for a mate. I once, to my astonishment, saw a pair carrying a larva each. This must have been exceptional, and it was not clear whether the female had intentionally collected the larva. Next day it had disappeared from her back, but unfortunately I was unable to observe whether or not it had been properly deposited.

Care of the young does not end when the father has deposited the larvae. These small frogs continue to supply the larvae, deposited in separate nurseries, with food eggs. The male lures a female to one of the larva-holding leaf vases and stimulates her to spawn. The eggs spawned in this way are fertilized and can develop further should the tadpole not consume them.

Finding a leaf vase with a larva in it seems to be less of a feat of memory on the part of the male than sheer luck. During his perambulations around his territory he seems to recognize which leaf vases contain larvae because of the conspicuous movements of the swimming larva (compare the breeding biology of *D. quinquevittatus*). This explains why some larvae are over-supplied with food while others starve.

As the larvae are not food specialists they will accept different kinds of food. This makes it easier to raise them artificially. Put them in solitary confinement in small plastic dishes, feed them with fish food, *Daphnia*, and gnat larvae, and they will develop to metamorphosis within about ten weeks. When the little frogs finally climb on land several days later they will be 10 mm (⅜ in) to 12 mm (½ in) long and superb miniature versions of their parents.

Dendrobates lehmanni (Plate 6)

Description *D. lehmanni* is closely related to *D. histrionicus*, with which it can crossbreed. But it is considered to be separate from *D. histrionicus* because its skin does not contain the specific histrionicus toxin. There are red and white striped specimens

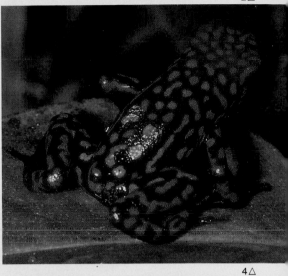

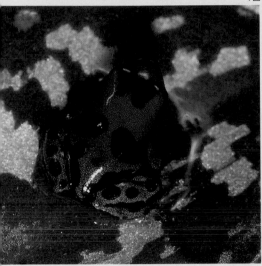

1 *D. auratus* (variation) from Taboga.
2 *D. azureus* (metamorphosing juvenile).
3 *D. fantasticus* (young).
4 *D. histrionicus.*
5 *D. imitator* with clutch.
6 *D. lehmanni.*

7 Pair of *D. azureus*.
8 *D. granuliferus*.

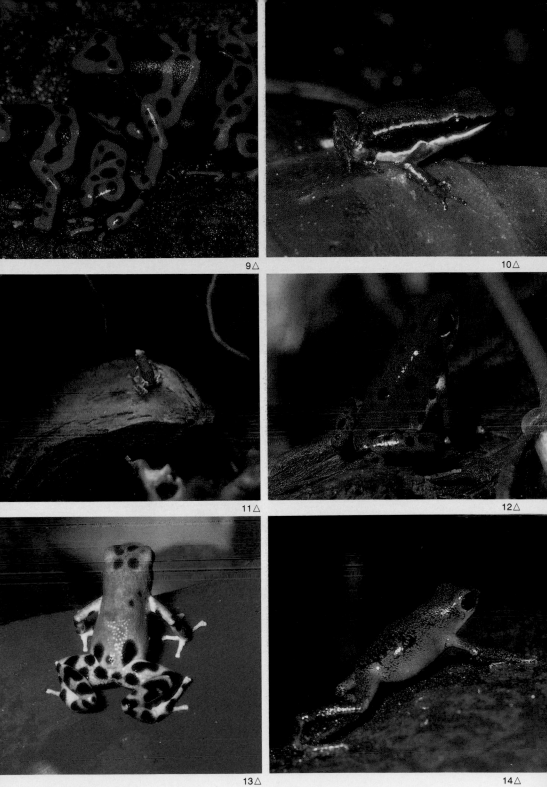

9 Pair of *D. leucomelas*.
10 *D. minutus*.
11 Strawberry poison-arrow frog (*D. pumilio*) in its natural habitat on the Bocas Islands.
12 Orange-red *D. pumilio* from the Bocas Islands.
13 Yellow *D. pumilio* from the same population on Bastimentos.
14 Blue *D. pumilio* from a neighbouring island.

15△

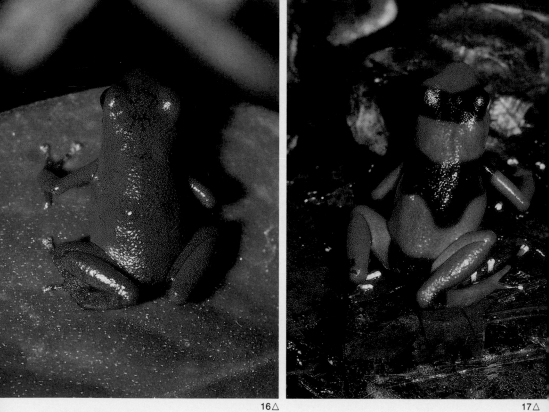

16△   17△

From The Bocas Islands:
15 Uniformly orange-red *D. pumilio* from Cayo Nancy.
16 Green-yellow *D. pumilio* from Shepard Island.
17 Yellow form of *D. histrionicus*.

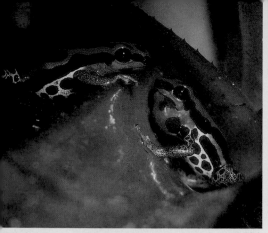

18△

19△

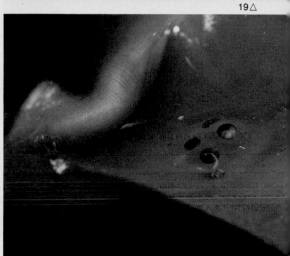

20△

21△

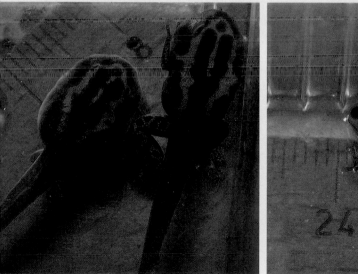

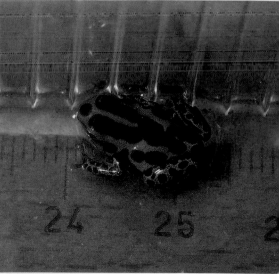

22△

23△

18 Male *D. quinquevittatus* in French Guiana coaxes the female closer with chirping calls.
19 Male changes over to a neighbouring leaf axil.
20 The frogs have moved into their breeding cave.
21 The pair have deposited a clutch of four eggs on the leaf they had carefully cleaned first.
22 By the time the front legs erupt the larvae have already changed colour.
23 The offspring a few days old.

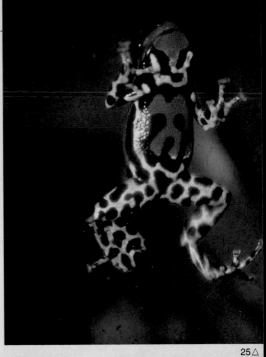

24△

25△

26△

24 A new form of *D. quinquevittatus* from Peru.
25 Underside of the new form of *D. quinquevittatus*.
26 *D. silverstonei*.

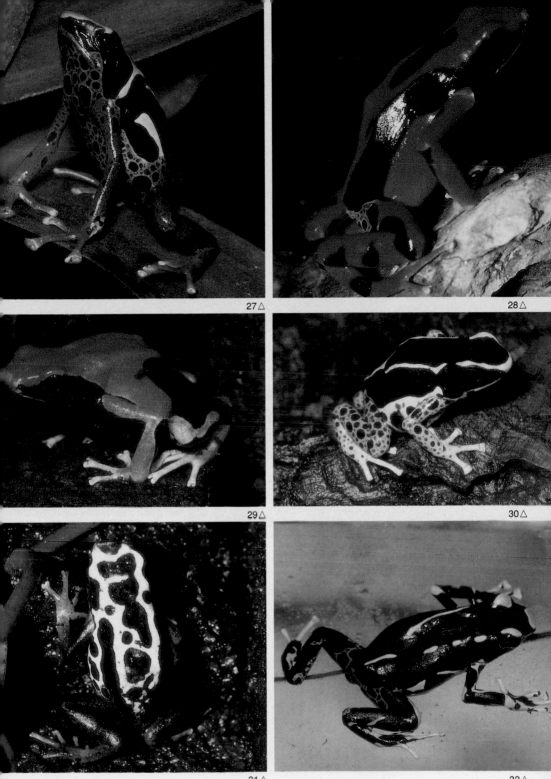

27 Yellow-blue *D. tinctorius* from coastal area, French Guiana.
28 Large yellow *D. tinctorius* from south-east French Guiana.
29 New yellow *D. tinctorius* from central French Guiana.
30 Black and white *D. tinctorius* from Surinam.
31 White reticulated *D. tinctorius* from the Oyapok.
32 Large black *D. tinctorius* from Surinam.

33 Small *D. reticulatus*; note contrast between glowing orange-red patterns and black and white reticulated pattern.

34△

35△   36△

34 *P. azureiventris*, easily recognizable by its light-blue belly.
35 *P. bassleri*, in transition to adult colouring.
36 *P. bicolor*, one of the most toxic of poison-arrow frogs.

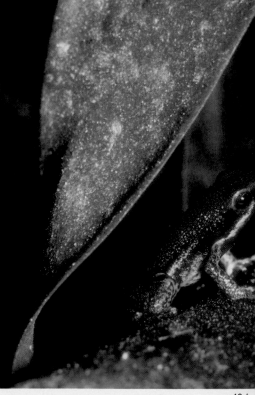

Four of the less conspicuously coloured poison-arrow frogs:
37 *P. femoralis.*
38 *P. lugubris* from Bastimentos.
39 *P. parvulus* (back view).
40 *P. parvulus* (side view).

41 *P. terribilis*, the most toxic animal in the world.
42 Young *P. terribilis* (right) compared in size with a young *D. quinquevittatus* (left).

43△

44△

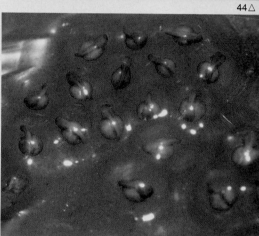

45△

46△

47△

48△

43 Calling *P. tricolor* male.
44 *P. tricolor* pair demonstrating *cephalic amplexus*.
45 *P. tricolor* clutch.
46 Development of the clutch by the fourth day.
47 Male carrying larvae.
48 Young *P. trivittatus*.

49 *P. vittatus* – easy to keep and breed.

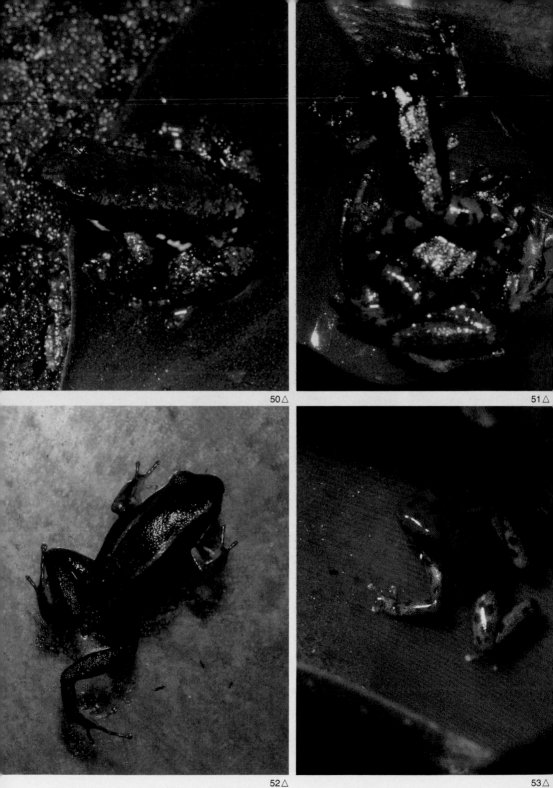

50△

51△

52△

53△

50 The Panama rocket frog (*C. inguinalis*).
51 Mating attempt by a pair of *C. saulii*.
52 *C. talamancae.*
53 Newly metamorphosed strawberry poison-arrow frog.

54△   55△

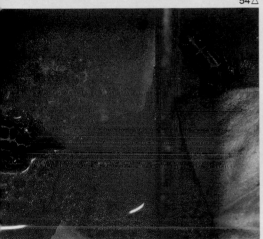

56△   57△

58△   59△

54 Strawberry poison-arrow frogs require bromeliad vases for reproduction.
55 Raising tadpoles in solitary confinement.
56 *D. imitator* during metamorphosis.
57 A young frog eating fruit flies dusted with a vitamin-calcium preparation.
58 A young *P. tricolor* with spindly-leg syndrome.
59 A tropical terrarium for poison-arrow frogs.

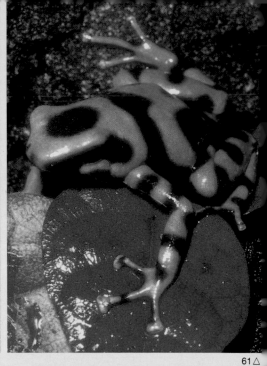

60△

61△

62△

60 *D. auratus* from Taboga.
61 A blue form of *D. auratus* from Panama.
62 A colour form of *D. tinctorius* from French Guiana.

with white or bluish toes as well as colour forms with yellow or orange cross bands on a black or brown background. The frog is similar in size to *D. histrionicus*, about 36 mm (1⅜ in).

Distribution and habitat These frogs live in high regions of Colombia, between 800 m (2,600 ft) and 1,200 m (4,000 ft), in damp forest areas combed by many watercourses.

Care in the terrarium Medium-sized terraria – about 70 cm (2 ft 3 in) by 60 cm (2 ft) by 50 cm (1 ft 8 in) – should be used. Humidity should be high. Temperatures need only be between 18° and 24°C. The frogs like to climb on leaves and bromeliads, so plants should be allowed to grow into the upper reaches of the terrarium. *D. lehmanni* has proved to be a rather sensitive species, which has until now been kept alive in terraria for only a few months. Imported frogs have tended to be infected with disease and in very bad shape. Once they have become acclimatized, though, they are easily kept and may even reproduce. So far *D. lehmanni* has taken no care of its young in the terrarium. The spawned eggs, which are deposited on bromeliad leaves or in spawning chambers, have to be taken out and artificially raised. The tadpoles should be fed with egg yolk in the same way as *D. histrionicus*.

Dendrobates leucomelas

(Plate 9)

A few years ago this sumptuously coloured frog was still a rarity in our terraria. Today it is more numerous and, pleasingly, most of the frogs now living in terraria have been bred in terraria – a successful result of committed terrarium keeping.

Description *D. leucomelas* is a medium-sized frog. The females can reach a size of around 4 cm (1½ in); the males remain a little smaller. Both sexes are varnished black with three yellow or orange cross bands distributed almost regularly across their backs. There are black blotches within the stripes. The extremities, too, are yellow or orange with black dots or bands, and the belly is black. Young frogs have to begin with three pure yellow cross bands – they only become mottled with black patterns later on.

Distribution and habitat The home of *D. leucomelas* is in Venezuela, where they inhabit the tropical rain-forests of the lowlands up to a level of 800 m (2,600 ft). They prefer the leaf litter on the forest floor and ground-level vegetation.

Care in the terrarium Medium-sized terraria are suitable. I keep five *D. leucomelas* in a glass terrarium measuring 70 × 70 × 45 cm (2¼ × 2¼ × 1¾ ft). *D. leucomelas* requires more warmth than *P. tricolor* – temperature should be between 24° and 30°C – and high humidity. Under these conditions the frogs will be in the mood for reproduction and the males will begin to call.

Outside the mating periods – usually occurring twice a year and lasting two to three months – the frogs will be quiet. Give them small insects as food, they are especially fond of caterpillars of the wax moth.

Behaviour and breeding Like all poison-arrow frogs *D. leucomelas* is active during the daytime, but leads a more hidden life than the related species *Phyllobates tricolor* and *D. auratus*. At first my frogs appeared only early in the morning and late in the afternoon, when they knew they would be fed. They now show themselves at other times, but still tend to retire often. A good portion of *Drosophila*, however, can lure them from hiding at any time of day. It is wonderful to see these shining yellow and black frogs slip out of hiding unexpectedly to secure their fair share of the meal.

Reproduction is initiated by a willing male, which will call out in the early hours of the morning with a long-drawn trilling lasting 10 to 15 seconds at a time. The calls become ever more penetrating with ever shorter pauses between them. The musician himself will be nowhere to be seen. In contrast to *P. tricolor* and the strawberry poison-arrow frog, which as a rule prefers lofty, conspicuous places, *D. leucomelas* produces his concerts from hiding. Usually the male will sit deep among dense plants and the female will have to take the initiative to coax him from his hiding place. She will nudge him from the rear and demandingly stroke him across his back with a front leg. Now the male will abandon his restraint and hop ahead, trilling away. The female will follow closely behind. It is up to the male to find a suitable spawning place. Usually he will decide quite quickly on a large spawning cave, formed from a clay flower pot, that he already knows. So he is able to find the entrance without delay and both frogs disappear inside. What goes on inside the spawning cave I do not know – my frogs have always interrupted their mating whenever I have disturbed them.

Towards evening I usually check the spawning cave. Generally I find a clutch of eggs deposited on oak leaves or on smooth plastic material. Usually there are five or six eggs, but I have found up to eleven.

In the wild the parent frogs would take care of the young from this point. The male would take the larvae to water on its back. But terrarium frogs have proved unwilling to look after their young according to the habits of their species, so there is nothing for it but to raise the clutches artificially.

Bringing up larvae and young frogs The eggs, which are quite large, about 4 mm (3/16 in), are deposited in a gelatinous mass. To begin with they are almost black, but they become lighter. On the fifth day the embryo is able to make its first movements and on the ninth it has developed into a tadpole with long, branching external gills and a still very large yolk supply. Given an ambient temperature of 25°C, the first tadpoles will emerge on the twelfth day. They still have their external gills, which disappear during the next two days.

The tadpoles are put in a small separate terrarium with water about 2 cm (3/4 in) deep. Tadpoles from one clutch can be raised together – I have not observed any cannibalism among them. If kept in water with much algae growth, and fed also on food flakes with a plant base, they will grow rapidly. After two weeks they will be 25 mm (1 in) long and after six, 35 mm (1 3/8 in) long. By then they will have developed back legs. Three weeks later the front legs will erupt. A few days later the young frogs will climb on to land. They will have three dirty yellow cross bands on their backs to begin with – only in a few days will the dull yellow intensify into a glowing yellow-orange.

The young frogs, which are about 15 mm (5/8 in) long to begin with, are raised in small terraria measuring 25 cm (10 in) × 20 cm (8 in) × 20 cm (8 in). In these small containers it is possible to feed them concentratedly on such foods as *Drosophila* and freshly hatched field crickets. These young frogs react very sensitively to lack of food – even two days without an adequate supply of food can lead to dangerous emaciation. The food insects should be dusted daily with a calcium-vitamin preparation, so that the frogs obtain sufficient minerals for their growth and a healthy development. The young frogs grow fast and are fully grown after less than a year.

Dendrobates minutus
(Plate 10)

Description *D. minutus* is the smallest species of poison-arrow frogs. The adult reaches a length only of 12 mm (½ in) to 16 mm (⅝ in). Silverstone (1975a) puts *D. altobueyensis, D. fulguritus, D. opisthomelas, D. quinquevittatus* and *D. steyermarki* in the same group as *D. minutus*. This is rather a plain frog. The dark brown of its slightly granulated back is broken only by two light-coloured side stripes. The top stripe runs from its eye to the bend in its back leg; the lower stripe runs parallel to this from the tip of its nose, below the eye, to the beginning of the back legs. The extremities contrast with the dark back – they are light brown to orange. In some populations the side stripes can be orange, golden, or yellow. The belly is usually lighter, with a whitish-blue marbled effect.

Distribution and habitat According to Silverstone (1975a), *D. minutus* lives at heights of 25 m (80 ft) to 1,098 m (3,600 ft), from central Panama to Columbia. The description above is of frogs from the high valley El Valle in Panama, at about 850 m (2,750 ft). I found them in the same habitat as *Colostethus inguinalis*, although further away from water in steep river-bank vegetation. They live on the ground between the roots of great trees, on rotting trunks, and in mossy rock clefts. Because of their brown camouflage colouring they are hard to find; if surprised they escape by quickly diving into the ground-cover vegetation.

Care in the terrarium Because they are very mobile, they need a terrarium that will give them a reasonable amount of space – one with a floor area of at least 60 cm (2 ft) × 40 cm (16 in). The floor should be broken up with many objects, such as stones, tree pieces, and roots, and from these flat areas as well as clefts and caves should be created. These frogs enjoy sitting among leaves, so the floor should be covered with a layer of oak-leaf litter. To determine the air temperature you have to know the frogs' place of origin – frogs from El Valle and other mountainous areas require temperatures of 18° to 24°C, but lowland dwellers need 22° to 27°C.

D. minutus will accept *Drosophila*, caterpillars of the wax moth (*Achroea grisella*), and other small insects as food. I have been unsuccessful in my attempts to breed *D. minutus* in a terrarium. They seem to be more difficult than other poison-arrow frogs. Clutches, which contained only one or two eggs, grew mould. According to Schulte (1980), the tadpoles should eat mosquito larvae and probably other foods as well. He reports the success of one terrarium keeper called Lee who raised a captured larva through to metamorphosis in 47 days – which indicates a period of development from egg to young frog of about 60 days. Schulte also reports that the frogs are sensitive to stress and dirt, but I cannot confirm this from observations of my own frogs. Presumably, the very small young frogs could not be raised successfully unless there was a well-functioning culture of springtails to act as a food supply.

Dendrobates pumilio
Strawberry poison-arrow frog   (Plates 11–16, 53, 54)

Not only because of its intense red colouring does the strawberry poison-arrow frog belong to the most conspicuous *Dendrobates* species. Its behaviour in caring for its young is also fascinating – the females feed their offspring with food eggs produced especially for the purpose.

Description *D. pumilio* is a small species with a length of 18 mm (¾ in) to 24 mm (1 in). Its colouring is very varied. The red form, which has given its name to the whole species, lives in Costa Rica. It has an intensely red back, covered in comma-shaped black dots, and black or deep blue legs. Frogs from western Panama, though, can be red, reddish-orange, blue, green, or olive-green and their bellies can be red, yellow, blue, or white. So confusing are the many different coloured forms that it is possible to believe that they represent different subspecies. The female is a little larger than the male. Some males show a darker coloured throat (vocal sac).

Distribution and habitat *D. pumilio* lives in the lowland forests of Central America, from northern Nicaragua, through Costa Rica, to western Panama. They are ground-dwelling frogs which will also climb around in low vegetation. Shulte (1980) reports that they live in cocoa plantations between fallen leaves, bromeliads, and stones on relatively sunny, restricted spaces.

Care in the terrarium Strawberry poison-arrow frogs can be kept well in terraria measuring 60 × 60 × 40 cm (2 × 2 × 1½ ft). Larger terraria are also suitable if a few pieces of banana are laid out so that the food insects (*Drosophila*) concentrate around them. Temperature should be between 25° and 30°C by day; at night, room temperature (20°C) is sufficient – as it is for other species too. Humidity should be high. When choosing plants, prefer the larger bromeliads, for the frogs like to sit in the vases, and they need them for reproduction. They will eat small field and house crickets, moths, and meadow insects as well as *Drosophila*.

Behaviour and breeding Strawberry poison-arrow frogs are active all day long, climbing around in the terrarium, searching for food. Reproduction is initiated by the male. Sitting in a high place, for example, a bromeliad leaf, it will give off penetrating 'epp-epp-epp' sounds. If a female is willing to mate, it will approach the calling male. He in turn will become 'nervous', begin to mince around on one spot, and signal to the female to follow him. Now he will look for a suitable place for spawning. Often the frogs will spawn on bromeliad leaves, near the water-filled leaf axils. My frogs from Costa Rica usually spawned on the ground among the oak-leaf litter, ignoring the spawning houses set up for other species.

After spawning has taken place, the four to eleven eggs are watered by the male. The tadpoles hatch after 10 to 12 days. They are so tiny – only 8–9 mm (5⁄16 in) – that they are known as pinheads.

Now the female will take over the care of the young. She will take the larvae on her back and carry them, usually individually, to water-filled bromeliad vases where she will deposit them. In the following weeks and months she will visit the larvae regularly and supply them with food eggs produced specially for this purpose. This feeding is continued until metamorphosis of the larvae. Sometimes, especially in larger terraria, you might not even notice your luck with breeding frogs. It seems like magic when, suddenly, tiny strawberry froglets, only 8 mm (5/16 in) long, stare up at you from bromeliad vases, and then dive down again quickly at any sign of danger.

Raising larvae and young frogs The artificial feeding of strawberry poison-arrow frogs is a tedious business. The larvae, specialized to live on food eggs, have so far accepted only chicken-egg yolk as a substitute. For feeding, the larvae are placed individually in small plastic dishes only a few centimetres in diameter. The water in these containers should be 2 cm (¾ in) to 3 cm (1¼ in) deep. The tadpoles are given just one drop of fresh egg yolk which, for example, can be allowed to drop from a matchstick into the water. Three hours later at most the water must be changed, otherwise the larvae would suffocate.

Compared to natural feeding with food eggs, the egg-yolk method has some drawbacks. First of all, the larvae grow only very slowly and take four to six months, a third longer than with natural feeding, to reach metamorphosis. And then, after this long effort, when the larvae finally reach the transformation stage, you may find that they have spindly legs syndrome and are therefore not viable. This means that the egg-yolk method is not ideal, though it seems to function sometimes. The young frogs have to be supplied with small insects (springtails), as they can manage *Drosophila* only after several weeks.

Dendrobates quinquevittatus (Plates 18–25, 42)

Description *D. quinquevittatus* is a small poison-arrow frog of about 16 mm (5/8 in) to 20 mm (¾ in). This species has very varied colouring. Specimens from French Guiana have a yellow and black pattern on their backs as a rule, while the belly and the legs appear silver-grey to greenish and have a pattern of black dots. The lemon-yellow throat is dotted in black also.

Populations from Peru are more in the yellowish-green range. One population is patterned with black dots; another displays a fine pattern of stripes. Bechter and Lescure (1983) describe a number of populations with different patterns of markings. They distinguish five forms – three striped, one transitional, and one dotted. There is also a red form which comes from Hameau Kuiru in Brazil. This is similar in appearance to *D. reticulatus*, except that it has two black stripes on its back.

Distribution and habitat *D. quinquevittatus* inhabits several countries of the Amazon area. According to Silverstone (1975a) it is native to Colombia, Peru, Ecuador, Brazil and French Guiana. This very wide distribution encourages the appearance of the differently coloured populations described above. It lives in damp forest areas, especially in peripheral zones bordering glades. Some populations are found near the ground, but others live in higher vegetation – for example, in bromeliads several metres up.

Care in the terrarium Although *D. quinquevittatus* is small it enjoys climbing and so should be given a roomy terrarium. Temperature should be between 24° and 28°C in the daytime and 18° to 22°C at night, with high humidity. Plant various types of bromeliads arranged in a stepped fashion so that the frogs can choose a bromeliad at the height of their choice.

I have been able to observe closely in the terrarium the reproductive behaviour of the striped form from French Guiana. In my terrarium, 80 × 50 × 50 cm (2½ × 1⅔ × 1⅔ ft), I keep a small group consisting of one male and three females. Three weeks after the frogs had been put in the terrarium, the male began to call, after I had misted up the terrarium with water spray. The call is very quiet and sounds like an insect rasping. Generally the calling male will sit on the leaf of a bromeliad (*Guzmania*) a few centimetres away from a leafy vase. If he catches sight of a female he will mince up the bromeliad leaf to show himself to her. A female willing to mate, recognizable by her rotund body, will hop towards him and try to make body contact. After they have climbed over one another a few times the male will hop to the spawning place, calling quietly to the female to follow him. The pair will climb from one leaf axil to the other – sometimes, if the male finally decides that the best spawning place is the leaf where he first sat and began calling, they will even make a complete circuit around the bromeliad. Both frogs wipe clean the chosen area of the leaf with their back legs. Then the male pushes himself backwards into the water-filled leaf vase, calling quietly. The female follows him, pushing her rear end into the vase beside him. As they squat side by side they are mating. The female begins to squeeze out from five to eight eggs. These squeezing movements obviously excite the male and it is presumably at this point that he releases sperm into the water. There is no clasping during mating. The male then leaves the spawning place, and the female remains alone. Often she will continue to produce eggs after the male has left. These late eggs must be fertilized by the sperm already in the water. The eggs develop during the next 10 to 14 days into ready-to-hatch tadpoles.

The male returns to the clutch only at the end of the developmental phase, when he checks that the clutch has not dried out. If it does seem dry he seems to be spurred on to extra effort when transporting the larvae. He normally picks up each tadpole individually, although Bechter and Lescure (1983) observed a male carrying up to five tadpoles at the same time – each one, though, was deposited separately in its own water-filled leaf vase. The male always makes sure that the chosen vase is not already inhabited by another tadpole. He recognizes an inhabited vase because the occupying tadpole will announce its presence by swimming around at the surface making shivering movements. This larval behaviour may have another purpose – it may be a way of begging for food. If it is successful the male will stay by the leaf vase and try to persuade a female to spawn there, thus providing food eggs for the larva. The eggs are fertilized so, if the larva dies and they are not required for food, they will carry on developing.

In 10 to 12 weeks the tadpoles' development is complete and young frogs measuring about 10 mm (⅜ in) and having the gorgeous colouring of their parents will leave the leaf vases.

Artificial feeding is not a problem – the larvae are not food specialists. I remove the clutch from the leaf during the first few days. This is quite a simple operation – you spray with water around the edges of the clutch until it detaches itself from the leaf and drops on to a plastic spoon held ready. The clutch is then kept in a small Petri dish with very little water to which a drop of mould inhibitor has been added. I transfer the hatched tadpoles singly into small plastic containers, like those used by do-it-yourselfers to hold screws or nails. As the larvae have a tendency to cannibalism, it is essential to raise them separately. They cannot even be raised together in an aquarium with a water content of several litres, as they excrete substances that seem to inhibit each others' growth into the water, so that the weaker larvae die in the end. Their food should consist of animal matter, such as gnat larvae, as they are mainly carnivorous. They begin to acquire their colouring early, when the back legs begin to form.

Dendrobates reticulatus (Plate 33)

Description *D. reticulatus*, at about 14 mm (½ in) to 16 mm (⅝ in), is among the smallest of poison-arrow frogs. It belongs to the *D. quinquevittatus* group (Zimmermann, 1983), which also includes *D. fantasticus* and *D. imitator*. Silverstone (1975a) regarded *D. fantasticus* and *D. reticulatus* as subspecies or forms of *D. quinquevittatus*, but according to more recent opinion (Myers, 1982) they constitute separate species.

D. reticulatus is conspicuously coloured. Its back is an intense orange-red which changes abruptly, towards the rear third, to a regular dot pattern on a blue-green background. The dot pattern is distributed also over the flanks, the belly and the extremities. The blue-green basic colour can be so suppressed by the black dots as to give the appearance of a green netted pattern on black. The females can be distinguished from the males only by their larger bodies. The young have a special juvenile colouring – two black stripes on their backs.

Distribution and habitat *D. reticulatus* lives congenially with *D. imitator*, *D. fantasticus* and the one-dot *D. quinquevittatus* in the Cordillera Central in north-eastern Peru. The frogs prefer the edges of the primary forest in glades or cleared woodland. They live on bromeliads, large-leafed plants in undergrowth, and on tree trunks, and will climb to heights of 2 m (6 ft) above the ground. They appear not to live higher than 800 m (2,600 ft) above sea level.

Care in the terrarium Because of its small size, *D. reticulatus* does not need a large terrarium – one measuring at least 60 × 40 × 30 cm (2 × 1½ × 1 ft) is adequate. It should be planted with bromeliads and creeping plants such as *Philodendron* and *Scindapsus*. These frogs appear to be sensitive to bacterial infections, so it is best to change daily the water held in the bromeliads and to remove dead plant matter immediately. The little frogs will be comfortable and, with luck, will reproduce with temperatures of 23°C at night and 27°C in the daytime and a high humidity of 90 per cent.

Reproduction behaviour is similar to that of *D. quinquevittatus*. For spawning the frogs will use the leaf axils of bromeliads but will also happily accept small black plastic containers (for example, film capsules) set at medium height in the foliage. *D. reticulatus* lays only small clutches of two or three eggs. As the clutches tend to grow mould, take them out of the terrarium as soon as possible and transfer them to small Petri dishes in which one drop of a mould inhibitor has been added to 5 ml (1 teaspoonful) of water. The larvae will accept food other than food eggs – raising them on, for example, gnat larvae and flake food works quite well. Because of their aggressive behaviour, they must grow up in solitary confinement.

Dendrobates silverstonei   (Plate 26)

Description *D. silverstonei* is one of the largest poison-arrow frogs – the females 43 mm (1¾ in), the males a little smaller. The granulated skin of the body is basically red or orange; the back generally has a pattern of black, irregular spots. The front legs are red like the body, the back legs black. Young have copper-coloured noses and are usually blackish-grey to begin with.

Distribution and habitat *D. silverstonei* lives in the Cordillera Azul in the Peruvian Andes. Schulte (1980) found the frogs in undisturbed mountain forest at 1,300 m (4,250 ft) to 1,800 m (6,000 ft) above sea level, the largest number at the forest edges. They are ground dwellers. In April air temperature was 22°C and water temperature 18°C. In its natural habitat *D. silverstonei* spawns in the months of May to July.

Care in the terrarium Because of the size of these frogs, the terraria in which they are kept must measure at least 70 × 70 × 50 cm (2¼ × 2¼ × 1⅔ ft). No more than two pairs should be kept in a terrarium of these dimensions – the males need rather large territories. Temperature should not rise above 25°C – these are frogs used to living in cool mountain forests. A pool of water in the terrarium, and a daily spray of water, will maintain high humidity. Food should consist of large insects such as moths (*Galleria mellonella*) and their caterpillars, medium-sized house crickets, and field crickets. The females deposit their clutches of up to 30 eggs in spawning houses. The larvae must be fed with egg yolk to begin with and later with flake food and insects.

Dendrobates speciosus

Description *D. speciosus* is a little larger than its close relative the strawberry poison-arrow frog (*D. pumilio*) – it measures about 30 mm (1⅛ in). The uniform shining red colour of its body and legs also distinguishes it from *D. pumilio*, as do its less prominent, or even non-existent, black markings. That these two species are closely related is proved by the fact that fertilized eggs and hatched tadpoles have been produced by a *D. pumilio* male with a *D. speciosus* female.

Distribution and habitat *D. speciosus* lives in mountainous areas between 1,100 m (3,600 ft) and 1,600 m (5,250 ft) above sea level in north-western Panama, and inhabits wet mountain forests.

Care in the terrarium *D. speciosus* should be kept in medium-sized terraria, which should be at least 60 cm (2 ft) high to cater for the frogs' need to climb. Temperatures should be 22° to 24°C by day and 18°C at night. These frogs need a high humidity, which can be maintained by spraying daily and by installing a small waterfall operated by a centrifugal pump. Reproductive behaviour is very similar to that of *D. pumilio*. The female will lay only a few eggs. After hatching she will carry the larvae individually to small bromeliad vases and feed them until metamorphosis with food eggs produced for this purpose. Artificial feeding of the larvae, which are specialized food-egg eaters, has to be done by the egg-yolk method described in detail for *D. pumilio*. Beutelschiess and Beutelschiess (1983) reported success with a food mixture of egg yolk, low-fat cottage cheese, soy flakes and a pinch of calcium-vitamin preparation. The development time from egg deposit to young frog was 157 days.

Dendrobates tinctorius

(Plates 27–32, 62)

Description *D. tinctorius* is one of the more spectacular species of poison-arrow frogs. Its size alone makes it stand out from all others – frogs from Surinam can be up to 60 mm (2⅜ in) long. The males remain smaller than the females and can be distinguished too by their enlarged, heart-shaped digital pads.

The colouring of these frogs varies with their place of origin. They display a yellow, yellow-orange, or white dorsal marking on a black base. Frogs from Surinam and French Guiana have a yellow-black back and flanks and deep blue legs; the belly is blue spotted with black. Other colour variations can be found in French Guiana, so it seems that *D. tinctorius* has developed a large number of forms.

Distribution and habitat *D. tinctorius* inhabits Guyana, Surinam and French Guiana and the bordering areas of Brazil. It lives in the lowland areas of the tropical rain-forests up to 400 m (1,300 ft) above sea level, usually among ground vegetation.

Care in the terrarium A terrarium for *D. tinctorius* should measure at least 70 × 70 × 45 cm (2¼ × 2¼ × 1½ ft). The temperature should be between 25° and 30°C and relative humidity 80 to 100 per cent. In their natural habitat the frogs live along the banks of streams, so we should offer them an artificial stream, run by a centrifugal pump, in the terrarium. Dense vegetation, of creepers, *Philodendron*, and large bromeliads, will not only look attractive but also create hiding places and a climbing apparatus for the frogs. They are greedy eaters and will not be satisfied with *Drosophila* alone. Field crickets, house crickets, and moths and their caterpillars should also be given.

Behaviour and breeding These big frogs are quiet creatures which spend nearly all day squatting in front of their hiding places. However, they become very active at feeding time. As a rule they keep to the lower reaches of the terrarium, but they will climb sometimes. At night they retreat into their caves or hide under plants.

In mating, the female is the active partner. When she is ready to mate she nudges the male continuously until he is roused. He reacts with quiet calls. Occasionally he will hop ahead and, by calling, encourage the female to follow him, but usually she will have to push hard to direct him to the spawning place. In the end, though, it is he who selects the spawning place, which in the terrarium will probably be the clay-pot house. When the female has deposited a clutch of 5 to 20 eggs she leaves the spawning house and it becomes the duty of the male to care for the clutch until the larvae hatch, which will be after 14 to 18 days. The larvae are about 15 mm (⅝ in) long.

Caring for larvae and young frogs The clutch should be removed from the terrarium for artificial feeding. The newly hatched larvae from a single clutch can be kept together in one breeding tank. Occasional mentions in the literature accuse them of cannibalism, but I have never observed it in tadpoles from one clutch.

My local water is hard and rich in calcium. If yours is soft follow the recommendation of Weygoldt (1982) and feed the larvae daily with a pinch of a calcium preparation.

The larvae are not difficult about their food. They will accept, among other things, flake food, algae, red-gnat larvae, and water fleas. The front legs erupt after three months. By then the larvae of the large Surinam frogs will have reached 4 cm (1½ in). At this point only a whitish-blue shading will indicate their later colouring. During the next two weeks the larvae will become coloured, the backs will become increasingly yellow and the legs and flanks will be offset in blue. After metamorphosis the young frogs will be 15 to 18 cm (⅝ to ¾ in) long. They should be raised in the usual fashion as described for *D. leucomelas*.

Other *Dendrobates* species

Species	Size	Appearance	Distribution	Special features
D. abditus	16–18 mm (⅝–¾ in)	Body black or dark bronze. Orange signal spots on armpits and groin. Mainly smooth skin.	Ecuador: Rio Azuela 1,700 m (5,600 ft)	Ground-dwelling. Larvae relatively large. Skin toxin has large quantities of pumilio-toxin A.
D. altobueyensis	15–17 mm (around ⅝ in)	Yellow, to gold, black dots on back	Colombia: Alto de Buey 980–1,070 m (3,200–3,500 ft)	Small species
D. arboreus	20–22 mm (¾–⅞ in)	Black or dark-brown, yellow spots on back and belly, skin lightly granulated	Panama: Rio Chiriquí 1,100–1,300 m (3,600–4,250 ft)	Lives in very high trees covered with bromeliads. Larvae raised in same way as *D. pumilio*. Skin toxin potent.
D. bombetes	16–20 mm (⅝–¾ in)	Back black with two red or orange stripes. Belly faint blue-green, green, or yellow. Legs partly red. Granulated skin.	Colombia: Cali 670–1,600 m (2,200–5,250 ft)	Ground-dwelling. Belongs to *D. minutus* group. Larvae mostly carried by female.
D. captivus	14–16 mm (½–⅝ in)	Brown with faint yellow or red spots. Skin not granulated.	Peru: Rio Santiago about 200 m (650 ft)	Mainly ground-dwelling. Very small species. Only a few specimens known so far.
D. fulguritus	13–17 mm (½–⅝ in)	Black with gold-yellow stripes.	Colombia: Chocó region 160–800 m (525–2,600 ft)	Very small species. Larvae in bromeliads.
D. galactonotus	30–40 mm (1⅛–1½ in)	Black with large, irregular yellow patterns or uniformly yellow back.	Brazil: Amazon 14–300 m (45–1,000 ft)	Large species. Belongs to *D. tinctorius* group.

Species	Size	Appearance	Distribution	Special features
D. maculatus	19 mm (¾ in)	Brown with yellow or red dots.	Panama: Rio Chiriquí	Very rare, only one specimen known.
D. mysteriosus	25 mm (1 in)	Brown with yellow dots. Flanks and belly granulated.	Peru: Alto Maranon 900 m (3,000 ft)	Only a few specimens known.
D. opisthomelas	14–20 mm (½–¾in)	Back red. Belly brown with red dots. Granulated skin.	Colombia: Cordillera Occidental, Cordillera Central 1,160–2,200 m (3,800–7,200 ft)	Highland species. Habitat sometimes at 10°C–12°C. Larvae in bromeliad axils.
D. steyermarki	16 mm (⅝ in)	Uniformly red, though sometimes with black dots.	Venezuela: Cerro Yapacana 1,200 m (4,000 ft)	Only a few specimens known.
D. truncatus	23–31 mm (⅞–1¼ in)	Black with gold-yellow to yellow-green stripes across the back.	Colombia: Rio Magdalena 100–1,133 m (325–3,700 ft)	Smallest species of D. tinctorius group. Bastard form with D. auratus possible.
D. vanzolinii	16–19 mm (⅝–¾ in)	Black, with yellow dots. Extremities bluish-grey patterned. Skin only slightly granulated.	Brazil. Peru: Pasco, Huanuco up to 1,300 m (4,250 ft)	Closely related to D. quinquevittatus.

11

The Genus *Phyllobates*

Phyllobates aurotaenia

Description According to Silverstone (1976), *P. aurotaenia* is a member of the *P. bicolor* group. The frogs look like enlarged *P. vittatus* – they measure 3 to 3.5 cm (1¼ to 1⅜ in) but have a plumper body. Their backs are matt black and are crossed by two green, yellow, or gold stripes. As a rule, there are no patterns on their equally black flanks. The belly, also black, displays a marbled pattern of green to blue. *P. aurotaenia* is one of the true poison-arrow frogs – its skin toxin is used as arrow poison by the Chocó Indians who live in the region of the Rio San Juan. It is, therefore, very toxic – care should be taken while handling it, and especially while handling captive wild specimens.

Distribution and habitat According to Silverstone (1976), *P. aurotaenia* inhabits the damp rain-forests of the Chocó area of Colombia, west of the Andes, up to 520 m (1,700 ft) above sea level, from the Rio Atrato in the north-east to the Rio San Juan in the south-west.

Care in the terrarium *P. aurotaenia* should be kept in medium-sized terraria with a floor area of about 70 × 40 cm (2¼ × 1½ ft). As it lives in the damp, hot lowlands of Colombia, it should be kept in high humidity and at a temperature between 22° and 28°C. Nothing is known about breeding in a terrarium, but it should mate like other members of the *P. bicolor* group. Silverstone (1976) describes the mating call as a loud, bird-like trilling lasting up to 45 seconds.

Phyllobates azureiventris (Plate 34)

Description This medium-sized poison-arrow frog was first described as *P. azureiventris* in 1985 by Kneller and Henle. The females reach a length of 27 mm (1 in); the males stay somewhat smaller. With its black back and golden-yellow dorsal stripes at the side it resembles *P. lugubris*, but can be distinguished by its additional golden yellow side stripes, which run from where the back legs begin to the shoulder and by the blue marbled marking on the throat, which *P. lugubris* only seldom displays.

Distribution and habitat Kneller and Henle (1985) found this new species on the eastern edge of the Peruvian Andes at 700 m (2,300 ft) above sea level. According to Kneller the frogs live in the primary forest, where they are ground dwellers, and are to be found in the leaf litter and low ground vegetation. Kneller reported a ground temperature of 24°C in their habitat.

Care in the terrarium *P. azureiventris* should be kept in a medium-sized terrarium with a floor area of about 60 × 40 cm (2 × 1⅓ ft). As the frogs are aggressive together, no more than two pairs should share a terrarium. The floor should be covered with a porous substance for drainage and this in turn covered with dry oak leaves. Roots, tree-trunk pieces, plants, and peat slabs can create hiding places for the frogs; a small body of water will complete the furniture. Kneller and Henle (1985) report that *P. azureiventris* deposited clutches of 12 to 16 dark grey eggs in a milky, opaque gelatinous substance under upturned coconut-shell halves or in the axils of bromeliads. The male guards them and carries the larvae together to water. Kneller was able to raise the larvae on algae, dead *Drosophila*, dead gnat larvae and a mineral preparation.

Phyllobates (Dendrobates) bassleri   (Plate 35)

Description *P. bassleri* is one of the larger species of poison-arrow frogs. Females attain a length of up to 45 mm (1¾ in); the males remain smaller. *P. bassleri* is black with a lemon-yellow head and back. The definition of the yellow areas can vary – some specimens look mainly yellow-orange with just an indication of a black marking, others have a yellow colouring only on their heads and upper back. The young animals are black to begin with, with two turquoise side stripes and have a little yellow around the head. Only later will the back slowly become lighter and more yellow.

Distribution and habitat According to Schulte (1981) *P. bassleri* inhabits a chain of mountains in Peru, where it is found in the damp mountainous forests. Schulte found most of the frogs at 700 m (2,300 ft) and 1,100 m (3,600 ft) above sea level. He found a higher population density in places where the woodland had been cleared. The creatures proved to be very shy.

Care in the terrarium The optimal terrarium size for *P. bassleri* is 70 × 70 × 50 cm (2¼ × 2¼ × 1⅔ ft). In keeping with the animals' lifestyle in mountainous regions, the temperature should not be too high – somewhere between 18° and 25°C.

I have had problems raising young *P. bassleri* – they would not grow properly and died after about six months, in spite of being given plenty of food dusted with vitamin-calcium. Possibly the day temperature of 28°C was too high.

P. bassleri will reproduce given high humidity and extra spraying. The clutches of 12 to 40 eggs are deposited in spawning houses on a smooth platic surface. The tadpoles are omnivorous, so raising them is easy.

Phyllobates bicolor
(Plate 36)

Description *P. bicolor* can attain a length of up to 4 cm (1½ in) and thus is one of the larger frogs in the genus *Phyllobates*. Silverstone (1976) included in the *P. bicolor* group *P. aurotaenia*, *P. lugubris*, and *P. vittatus*. *P. terribilis*, which obviously was not known to Silverstone when he compiled his grouping, also belongs to the group. The close relationship of the species in the group is demonstrated in, among other things, the colouring of the young, which look astonishingly alike with their black backs and golden-yellow dorso-lateral stripes.

Adult specimens of *P. bicolor* have a uniformly red, orange-red, or yellow back. The extremities and the belly are usually black. Some frogs, however, have an orange-yellow or golden-yellow belly. They then look very similar to *P. terribilis* and often cannot be distinguished from it except with knowledge of where they were found. The skin secretions of *P. bicolor* are very poisonous, but toxicity declines dramatically after a long time in a terrarium – as does that of *P. terribilis*.

Distribution and habitat *P. bicolor*, according to Myers and Daly (1983a, b), lives in western Colombia, from the Chocó region to the area drained by the Rio San Juan. Like *P. terribilis*, it is a ground-dwelling frog which will not climb above ground vegetation level. According to Silverstone (1976) it is distributed over heights from 25 m (80 ft) to 1,525 m (5,000 ft) above sea level.

Care in the terrarium *P. bicolor* will feel comfortable in a terrarium with a large floor area at high humidity and temperatures between 22° and 26°C. Other conditions of care are similar to those of *P. terribilis*.

Phyllobates (Dendrobates) femoralis   (Plate 37)

Description *P. femoralis* is one of the less conspicuously coloured poison-arrow frogs. They are shiny brown to brown-black on top, with a light-coloured dorso-lateral stripe running from the nose over the eyes to the beginning of the back legs. Another white stripe runs parallel to the first underneath the eyes. This stripe separates the dark back and flanks from the lighter brown-white marbled colour of the belly. The extremities are light-brown and in some populations have a reticulated pattern. The iris of the eyes is brown. The frogs are 22 to 28 mm (⅞ to 1⅛ in) long.

Distribution and habitat According to Silverstone (1976), *P. femoralis* inhabits the damp, low-lying forests of Guyana, Surinam, and French Guiana and the Amazon regions of Colombia, Ecuador, Peru and Brazil. Silverstone reports 610 m (2,000 ft) above sea level as their upper limit. In French Guiana they are found in forest areas on the ground and in low vegetation. When threatened they disappear into the leaf litter like lightning, with great leaps.

Care in the terrarium *P. femoralis* requires a medium-sized terrarium with a floor area of at least 50 × 50 cm (1⅔ × 1⅔ ft).

To duplicate the natural habitat of the frogs as nearly as possible the terrarium should be furnished to look like a forest floor, with sheets of peat moss, root chunks, and oak leaves, and be planted in several levels. The frogs will not feel comfortable in a light terrarium and will make panic-stricken attempts to escape. Schulte (1980) reports that they are very sensitive to stress, but I have not observed this in my specimens from French Guiana. A small stream with filter pump will complete the scene and heighten the well-being of our frogs. Air temperature should lie between 22° and 30°C and be combined with high humidity. *P. femoralis* is not choosy about food – it will eat anything from the tiniest insects such as *Drosophila* to medium-sized house crickets.

Schlüter (1987) observed heightened activity and saw males carrying larvae, at the beginning of the rainy season (October) in Panguana, Peru, when the daily rainfall reached about 30 mm (1⅛ in). For these frogs then, and for those from French Guiana, t ie beginning of the rainy season is a stimulant to mating. For breeding attempts, therefore, a rainy season should be simulated in the terrarium by raising the temperature and spraying v ith water in February or March. According to Schulte (1980), in Ecuador the spawning period of *P. femoralis* falls in the months of April to June, whereas in Surinam it lasts from June to July.

Mating is initiated by the male with constant trilling sounds. The mating ritual is similar for all members of the *P. femoralis* group, in which Silverstone (1976) includes *P. anthonyi*, *P. boulengeri*, *P. espinosai*, *P. tricolor* and *P. zaparo*.

Phyllobates lugubris (Plate 38)

Description These small frogs look very similar to *P. vittatus*, but will remain about 5 mm (³⁄₁₆ in) smaller, at 25 mm (1 in). Their upper parts, like those of *P. vittatus*, are shiny black but their two yellow or orange dorso-lateral stripes are narrower than those of *P. vittatus*. Below the eyes a light-coloured stripe on the nose runs along both sides. The belly, excluding the dark throat area, is marbled blue-black; the extremities show a greenish or bronze-coloured glow which can swamp the black marbled effect almost completely.

Distribution and habitat *P. lugubris* inhabits the lowlands and the temperate mountain slopes on the Caribbean side of Costa Rica and Panama up to 650 m (2,100 ft) above sea level, according to Silverstone (1976). The frog shown in plate 38 came from Bastimentos, one of the Bocas Islands of Panama, where *P. lugubris* inhabited a strip of forest with dense ground vegetation near the coast, sharing its territory companionably with *Coloste-thus talamancae* at the edge of a large population of *D. pumilio*.

Care in the terrarium These attractive little frogs will feel comfortable in a fairly small terrarium – a floor area of about 50 × 40 cm (1⅔ × 1¼ ft) is sufficient – as long as it is densely planted with different bromeliads and creeping plants. For lowland frogs the temperature should be about 28°C during the day and about 22°C at night. Frogs from higher areas are kept in a slightly cooler environment.

On the whole, *P. lugubris* is an easy frog to keep in the terrarium. Given reasonable luck it can be encouraged to reproduce. The clutches of 12 to 20 eggs are deposited on bromeliad leaves or in spawning houses. During the following 12 to 16 days, until the tadpoles hatch, the father will visit the clutch regularly in order to moisten it. Generally he will pick up the hatched larvae together and carry them piggyback to a suitable body of water. He gives no further care to the young. The tadpoles should at this stage be removed from the terrarium and transferred to a small aquarium. If they are well fed with flake food, food tablets, and defrosted gnat larvae they should reach metamorphosis after about eight weeks. After the emergence of their front legs, at the latest, they should be given an opportunity to climb on land. It is a good idea to float a few pieces of cork oak on the surface of the water to provide artificial islands for the young frogs to use.

The new young frogs, which will have a length of 1 cm (⅜ in) or more, should be transferred to a well-prepared breeding terrarium. This can be quite spartanly furnished – a foam mat, which should be kept constantly damp, as a floor covering and a few peat moss slabs or some chunks of cork-oak bark to provide hiding places are all that is needed. For plants I usually use cuttings of *Scindapsus* which are very hardy and can even be washed down with warm water. Plenty of food, including small

Drosophila, freshly hatched house crickets, and small wax-moth caterpillars, all dusted with vitamin-calcium, will ensure that the juveniles grow quickly and will be fully grown after about one year.

Phyllobates (Dendrobates) parvulus (Plates 39, 40)

Description *P. parvulus* is a small frog with a length of around 24 mm (1 in). Myers *et al.* (1978) assigned the species, together with *P. pictus*, *P. pulchripectus*, *P. petersi* and others, to the genus *Dendrobates*. Silverstone (1976) included it in *Phyllobates*. Classification on the basis of skin toxins, as attempted by Myers *et al.*, did not prove very useful, as the composition of the skin toxin can change (for example, in the case of later generations of animals in captivity).

P. parvulus is an attractive little frog, although it has no conspicuous colouring. The bronze colour of the lightly granulated back changes along the flanks to a shining black, which in turn is broken up by a whitish-blue marbling where the back legs begin. Above the front legs a white band stretches along the lips to the tip of the nose. Like *P. pictus*, *P. parvulus* has yellow spots in its armpits and groin. The extremities are brownish and look less strongly granulated than the back.

Distribution and habitat According to Silverstone (1976), *P. parvulus* inhabits the Amazon regions of Colombia, Ecuador and Peru, east of the Andes. The frogs live in forest areas in the lowlands and at elevations of up to 1,000 m (3,300 ft).

Care in the terrarium A terrarium with a floor area of about 50 × 40 cm (1⅔ × 1¼ ft) is big enough for these small frogs. The living conditions in the terrarium should be similar to those for *P. pictus*. Newly metamorphosed young frogs are very small and have to be fed with springtails or similar tiny insects for the first ten weeks.

Phyllobates (Dendrobates) pictus

Description *P. pictus* is one of the smallest of the *Phyllobates* – females will reach 28 mm (1⅛ in), males a maximum of 25 mm

(1 in). Its colouring is not conspicuous. The back is brownish-black, slightly granulated. A white to cream dorso-lateral band runs from the beginning of the back legs to the tip of the nose and a second, shorter stripe runs from the beginning of the front legs to the nose. (As *P. femoralis* also has these stripes, the two species can hardly be distinguished from each other visually.) The extremities are offset in brown. Orange-red spots are displayed in the armpits and groin, though when the animal is resting these marks can scarcely be seen. The belly is a dark colour and displays a lighter marbling increasing towards the rear.

Distribution and habitat According to Silverstone (1976) *P. pictus* inhabits an enormous area – almost the entire region drained by the Amazon. It can be found in Guyana, Surinam, French Guiana, Venezuela, Colombia, Ecuador, Peru, Bolivia, Brazil and northern Paraguay. Its habitat is the damp rain forests of the lowlands. Here it lives on the forest floor and climbs on fallen trees and low vegetation. According to Silverstone (1976), it can be found up to 915 m (3,000 ft) above sea level.

Care in the terrarium The fast-moving *P. pictus* can be kept in a medium-sized terrarium (with a side length of 60 cm, 2 ft) at a temperature between 22° and 28°C and in high humidity. The floor covering, which should be kept constantly damp, can be a porous substance covered with a layer of leaf litter or slabs of peat moss covered with growing moss. A small pool of water, fed by a stream with a filter pump, pieces of bark, and plants will complete the furnishings. The plants should include a few bromeliads, as the frogs like to spawn on their smooth leaves.

Under these conditions breeding in the terrarium is quite simple. According to Weygoldt (1983) *P. pictus* will keep up its mating call, consisting of quick, sharp 'tick-tick-tick' sounds, for hours. The mating pair performs the same kind of cephalic clasping as does *P. tricolor*. The clutch contains 20 to 30 eggs, each having a diameter of 2 mm (1/32 in). During the following two weeks the male looks after the clutch and supplies it regularly with moisture. The hatched larvae are carried together piggyback to a suitable body of water and deposited.

Weygoldt (1983) reports that raising the tadpoles is not difficult. As detritus-eaters they can be fed with algae, fish food, and dried yeast flakes.

Newly metamorphosed young frogs will be about 10 mm (3/8 in) long. The tiny froglets should be kept in a small breeding terrarium and fed at first on springtails and mites. After a few weeks they will be able to manage small *Drosophila* and from then on vitamins and minerals should be added to the food (by dusting the food insects with mineral powder) so that the young frogs will grow into strong specimens of the next generation. As *Phyllobates* individuals are quite peaceable together the young frogs can be raised in the terrarium with their parents from the age of a few months onward.

Phyllobates terribilis   (Plates 41, 42)

Description *P. terribilis*, like *P. aurotaenia* and *P. bicolor*, is a poison-arrow frog that carries its name by right. The Chocó Indians of Colombia even today poison their blow-pipe arrows with the skin toxin of these frogs.

The question has to be asked whether these very venomous frogs are suitable at all for keeping in a terrarium, or whether they can become a lethal danger to their keepers. *P. terribilis* is armed with the strongest non-protein toxins known. Analysis has established that a single *P. terribilis* produces enough batrachotoxin and homobatrachotoxin to kill 20,000 mice or 10 humans. Luckily for us, though, the toxicity of these frogs is reduced quite considerably when they are kept in the terrarium. After one year the frogs are only half as toxic, and following generations of these 'poison dwarves' seem not to have a trace of poison left, according to investigations by the scientists (compare Zimmermann and Zimmermann 1985a). Why this should be so is not known. But it does mean that keeping later generations of this terrible poison frog does not seem to carry any risk. None the less, you may well think *P. terribilis* too dangerous for the amateur terrarium.

P. terribilis, being almost 5 cm (2 in) long, is one of the larger poison-arrow frogs. Its colouring is a uniform yellow, yellowish-green, or orange. The extremities and the belly are only slightly darker than the other parts of the body. Animals that are clearly a darker colour on their back legs and belly are probably not

P. terribilis but *P. bicolor*, which can, however, be distinguished by its yellow back and because it is bigger.

Young frogs have a different, juvenile, colouring; they are black with lateral yellow stripes on their backs – a colouring that makes them resemble juveniles of *P. vittatus*.

Distribution and habitat *P. terribilis* lives in western Colombia and, according to Myers and Daly (1983), is found only in a small area around the Rio Saija. *P. aurotaenia* and *P. bicolor* are not found as far south as that, so knowledge of where a specimen was found is helpful in determining the species.

Schulte (1980) describes the habitat of the terrible poison frog as being untouched, hilly, lowland rain-forest at about 200 m (650 ft) above sea level. The frogs are said to live mainly on the forest floor, on damp slopes or near rivers. Population density appears not to be high, as Myers only seldom found two animals near each other.

Care in the terrarium Keeping this large species requires a suitable roomy terrarium, one with a floor area of about 60 × 50 cm (2 × 1⅔ ft). The whole set-up should be viewable from above. There should be some empty areas on the floor. A large bromeliad in a pot and a few tree roots should be provided as hiding places for the frogs. In the background, height can be given to the terrarium landscape by planting such creepers as *Scindapsus*. A small pool of water is necessary; the frogs will need it to deposit their larvae. They prefer air temperatures of between 22° and 28°C, with high humidity. Feeding is not difficult, as the frogs eat large *Drosophila*, house crickets, field crickets, wax moths, and other insects.

Breeding, too, is easy. The sight of a plump female ready to spawn spurs the male to frenetic activity. He voices his enthusiasm with a long-drawn-out trilling sound. This long-distance courting call, described by Zimmermann and Zimmermann (1985b), usually induces the female to approach the male. When she is within a few centimetres of him, he hops towards her. She strokes her front legs across his back and rubs her flanks against his. He breaks away from her to hop off to a spawning place and she follows. Occasionally he utters a quiet mating call, the short-distance mating call (Zimmermann and Zimmermann,

1985b), but it seems unnecessary – the female is aroused enough to follow anyway. The pair finally disappear into the spawning house, an upside-down flower pot with a small entrance hole resting on a smooth surface, such as a Petri dish. After one or two hours the male emerges. The female remains behind and spawns in his absence. Whether the male deposits sperm on the spawning area before the eggs are deposited or whether he fertilizes the eggs later, when the female has left, I am unable to say. At any rate the male will go back to the spawning place again, after the female has left it.

The clutch consists of up to 30 eggs, which are deposited with much gelatinous substance, and are therefore well protected against drying out. The male will not care for the clutch during the following days. Nor will he moisten the clutch, as other poison-arrow frogs are known to do. After two or three weeks the tadpoles burst their egg membranes. Now the father is recalled to his duties and sets out to find the clutch. He squats on the gelatine among the hatched larvae and flattens himself so that the larvae can slither along his flanks to his back. As a rule he makes several trips carrying larvae, until all have been deposited in a water-filled plastic dish on the terrarium floor.

The larvae can be raised without problems in small aquaria. They are quite peaceable, so the larvae from one clutch can normally be raised together. If the clutch is a large one, though, it is advisable to distribute the larvae over several tanks. The tadpoles are omnivorous, so feeding them is no problem – they will accept everything from flake food to gnat larvae. With adequate food and a regular change of water they will reach metamorphosis in eight to ten weeks.

Care is necessary now. The young, 10 mm (⅜ in)-long, frogs are extremely sensitive to dirt in their breeding container. Zimmermann and Zimmermann (1985b) report early failures in raising young, apparently because the breeding tanks were not kept scrupulously clean. In order to be able to clean the tank more easily it is best to use a foam-rubber mat as a floor covering. On top of this mat, which should be kept damp all the time, I usually lay a few cork chunks as hiding places for the frogs. For plants I recommend young shoots of the ivy *Scindapsus*, which will root easily in the damp foam mat. The recipe for the successful raising of *P. terribilis* is weekly cleaning of the breeding tank. Everything in the tank must be washed in hot water.

The young frogs should be given a mineral powder daily (by dusting the food insects) to provide them with sufficient minerals (calcium) for healthy bone formation.

After 18 to 20 months the young frogs will have grown to adulthood. As a second or subsequent generation they are just as attractive as the members of their species living in the wild, but luckily they are not nearly so toxic.

Phyllobates (Dendrobates) tricolor   (Plates 43–47, 58)

P. tricolor is a very recommendable poison-arrow frog. It is easy to keep, has an attractive colouring, and its liveliness makes it stand out from all other Dendrobatides. All year round the male of this species will show its readiness to mate by constant trilling.

Description At about 2.5 cm (1 in) *P. tricolor* is one of the smaller species. It has a basic dark, usually cinnobar-red colour, and as a rule displays three yellow-white long stripes, which can also be present in a very faint version. The belly and extremities are a basic red with either yellow-white spots or marbling. Unfortunately, these beautiful light stripes seem to disappear in later generations of terrarium-bred frogs, as they become narrower from generation to generation. The females are plumper and larger than the males.

Distribution and habitat *P. tricolor* lives in Ecuador, on the Pacific side of the Andes at heights of 1,200 m (3,900 ft) to 1,800 m (5,900 ft) above sea level. The frogs live near water, along small rivers or streams, although their habitat also includes dry areas.

Care in the terrarium For these small frogs a terrarium measuring 60 × 60 × 40 cm (2 × 2 × 1¼ ft) is sufficient. Temperature should be around 24°C, although higher temperatures will not harm the frogs. At a high relative humidity of 80 to 100 per cent they will be ready to mate all year round – so much so that unless they are given occasional dry spells they will burn themselves out too quickly in their constant mating fury. They live on the ground but also like to climb, so the terrarium should be furnished with broad-leaved plants for them to spend time on. They will eat *Drosophila*, small field crickets, house crickets, wax moths and caterpillars.

Behaviour and breeding Probably no other species is as eager to reproduce. In the early hours of the morning the male heralds his presence with a high trilling sound which seems irresistible to the females. When a willing female approaches the calling male, he doubles his efforts and trills so hard that his whole body vibrates. Then he becomes silent, hops forward a few paces, and calls again. The female turns to him and he now hops ahead of her, still trilling. She follows closely, trying hard to make body contact. This 'chase' can last for a while, until the male has found a suitable spawning place.

Usually the pair disappear into their spawning cave – a small flower pot laid on its side, with its opening disguised with a few leaves, so there is only a small entrance. Inside, the male will climb on to the female's back and clasp her around the neck with his front legs. The pair sometimes remains in this position for hours. Then the female squeezes out 15 to 40 eggs in several thrusts. Usually the eggs are immediately fertilized by the male, but sometimes he will leave the female before she has spawned, returning afterwards to find the clutch she has left behind and, presumably, to fertilize it. From now on, the male cares for the offspring. He waters the clutch and defends it very aggressively. He utters territorial calls and drives off intruders by jumping on them, grabbing their heads, or squeezing them in a sort of bear hug.

After 10 to 14 days the tiny tadpoles hatch, leave their egg coverings, and lie on the gelatinous membranes. The father squats in the membranes, creates a hollow back, and allows them to climb on to it. Then he carries them to a suitable pool of water. He is very fussy about his choice of water, often carrying the tadpoles around for several days. Depositing the tadpoles is his last act in caring for his young.

For the next stages of breeding the tadpoles can be left in the water in the terrarium or can be taken out. Usually, it is advantageous to transfer the larvae to special breeding tanks, as it is easier to feed and check them there.

Raising the larvae and young frogs Usually it is best to take the clutches out of the terrarium immediately after spawning. In my terraria, which usually house many frogs, it has happened that, in spite of the male's attempts to defend the eggs, they have been damaged or even eaten by other frogs. And sometimes the terrarium keeper cannot find where the male has deposited the tadpoles, so that purposeful breeding becomes impossible. Artificial breeding means one can check the clutches better and mould attack can be prevented or inhibited.

My frogs usually spawn in the little spawning houses set up for this purpose. These can be clay pots or half coconut shells, with small holes made for entry. They are set on a smooth plastic or glass base, or dry oak leaves are scattered inside. After the frogs have spawned, clutch and base can be removed together. The clutch is transferred to a small plastic box containing a little water. The clutch should touch the water and should be sprayed with water once or twice a day.

Fertilized clutches develop into free-swimming tadpoles within 10 to 16 days. On the second day a whitish, circular dot appears on the dark-coloured eggs. This indicates the yolk stage. Eggs that are white right through have to be removed – they are unfertilized and can attract mould that will invade the whole clutch. Mould, in fact, is an ever-present danger. It can destroy the clutch. An anti-fungal substance, therefore, should be added to the water in the breeding vessel. The embryos will begin to move after five days. After seven days they can be recognized as tadpoles with external gills. Further care of the tadpoles should take place in small breeding tanks. As the larvae of *P. tricolor* are not aggressive, they can be raised together. The water level in the breeding tank should be only 2 cm (¾ in) to begin with, so that the larvae can reach the surface quickly. Later it can be raised to 10 cm (4 in). The breeding tank needs only a few water plants and dry oak leaves for the larvae to hide under.

Feed them with fish food, algae, pieces of beef heart, and defrosted red-gnat larvae. The larvae will grow fast in water at between 20° and 25°C. After six or seven weeks they will have attained their final length of about 30 mm (1⅛ in). Then metamorphosis will be complete.

When their front legs have emerged, tadpoles have to be able to leave the water and find land, otherwise they will drown. The simplest answer is to tip the breeding tank slightly so that the lower part is filled with water and the upper parts become dry. I have never come across a drowned young frog with this method. Now, at the latest, is the time to cover the tank with a piece of glass or plastic foil, to ensure high humidity and prevent the frogs escaping.

The young frogs live off the substance in their stumpy tails for the first few days. They are at first about 10 mm (3/8 in) to 12 mm (1/2 in) long and an uninteresting brown colour. It will take another few months before they are as beautiful as their parents.

To begin with I keep these young *P. tricolor* in small breeding terraria furnished with moss, a few small plants, and cork pieces. They eat springtails, mites, and small *Drosophila*, which I first dust with a calcium-vitamin preparation. After six months the males begin to voice their first, somewhat unsure calls. In a year the frogs will be fully grown.

P. tricolor is a prolific species. A single female of my stock managed to spawn seven times in three months and produced 139 eggs, an average of 20 eggs per clutch. (Projected for a year that would result in about 600 eggs from a single pair.) Sadly, though, all the young she produced suffered from spindly leg syndrome.

Phyllobates (Dendrobates) trivittatus (Plate 48)

Description *P. trivittatus* is one of the largest poison-arrow frogs. The females can attain a length of up to 50 mm (2 in); the males are visibly smaller. *P. trivittatus* has a matt black basic colour on its back, which is edged by two lateral lemon-yellow stripes. The legs are greenish, the belly black with green or blue marbling. Very beautiful, but rare, are specimens that have a glowing green back instead of a black one.

Distribution and habitat *P. trivittatus* can be found in the lowland forests of South America, in Guyana, Surinam, French Guiana, Colombia, Ecuador, Peru, and Brazil. The frogs live on the forest floor between palm roots or stilt roots or in the thickets of fallen trees. They are very shy and because of their dark colouring can be seen only with difficulty in their habitat.

Care in the terrarium *P. trivittatus* acclimatizes best in a terrarium measuring at least 80 × 70 × 50 cm (3 × 2¾ × 1⅔ ft). The terrarium should be thickly planted, to give the frogs, which will be very shy at first, plenty of hiding places. Another reason is that *P. trivittatus* can jump about quite violently and in too thinly planted terraria the occupants tend to bash their noses against the glass, sometimes so hard as to injure themselves. Mating is initiated by the males, which call out from a high position. The females deposit up to 30 eggs in spawning houses or on leaves. The larvae hatch after 14 to 18 days and metamorphose in 6 to 8 weeks. The young frogs are only 15 mm (⁹⁄₁₆ in) long at first. They eat algae, dried food, and gnat larvae. It is important that they get enough vitamins and minerals, so the food insects should be dusted with mineral powder.

Phyllobates vittatus

(Plate 49)

This beautiful little frog has for years been for terrarium keepers one of the most popular poison-arrow frogs, not least because it is easy to keep and easy to breed.

Description The female *P. vittatus* attains a length of up to 29 mm (1⅛ in); the male is smaller. *P. vittatus* is thus some 3 to 5 mm (⅛ to ³⁄₁₆ in) longer than *P. lugubris*, which is almost identical in appearance. On a black basic colour it displays two lateral stripes across the tip of its nose, the head, and back. The stripes can be golden, yellow, or yellow-orange. The back is broken up by a number of turquoise to gold spots, which run along the centre of the back. This pattern of spots is clearer in the female; in the male it can even be completely absent.

Distribution and habitat *P. vittatus* inhabits the lowland forests on the Pacific side of Costa Rica. Its territory is the vegetation near the ground – it does not climb as high as other species.

Care in the terrarium The terrarium should measure at least 60 × 60 × 40 cm (2 × 2 × 1⅓ ft). Temperature by day should be between 24° and 30°C and by night 20°C. A built-in stream will ensure high humidity, which can be raised to satiation limit by additional spraying. The frogs will eat *Drosophila*, young field crickets, and house crickets and will particularly enjoy small moths. When furnishing the terrarium with plants it is important to include bromeliads – the frogs will use their wide, smooth leaves for spawning.

Behaviour and breeding The males display marked territorial behaviour. A male entering the territory of another male will be attacked; the defending male jumps on the intruder's back and squeezes him in a bear hug.

P. vittatus seems to reproduce all year round. The males keep up a constant high trilling to attract females willing to mate. When a female approaches the male trills even more loudly and makes visual signals – rearing up, mincing around on the spot, or dancing in a circle. The aroused female strokes the male's back several times. Then the male will look for a suitable spawning place. It hops ahead with the female following closely. Finally the pair will find a suitable bromeliad leaf. The female will deposit the eggs while the male squats opposite her and waits. No clasping takes place during spawning.

After the female has deposited her clutch of 7 to 20 eggs, she hops away. The male sits on the clutch and fertilizes the eggs. During the next 13 to 16 days he looks after the clutch and keeps it moist. When the larvae, measuring about 12 mm (½ in) hatch, the male carries them piggyback to search for a suitable pool of water to drop them in. According to observations made by M. Schmidt (1983) it can take up to eight days before the last larvae are deposited – the tadpoles begin to grow on the father's back and become visibly larger before they are deposited.

Caring for larvae and young frogs If the aim is to raise the larvae under controlled conditions the clutches should be removed for artificial rearing. The water in the breeding container should have a mould inhibitor added to it right from the start to prevent mould formation. If the father is already carrying his offspring on his back, it is possible to catch him together with his young and place them all in a small breeding tank containing 2 to

3 cm (¾ to 1¼ in) of water. Usually, the male will deposit at least some of the tadpoles.

Caring for the tadpoles is not difficult. Feed them on algae, dried food, red-gnat larvae, and water fleas. At temperatures between 20° and 25°C the tadpoles reach metamorphosis after about 40 days. The young frogs can be fed with small *Drosophila* and freshly hatched field and house crickets. It is especially important to dust the food insects with mineral powder, otherwise the young frogs will grow deformed or dwarfed. Given a good varied diet they should be fully adult after a year.

Other *Phyllobates* species

Species	Size	Appearance	Distribution	Special features
P. anthonyi	20 mm (¾ in)	Dark brown with three light-coloured dorsal stripes	South-west Ecuador to north-west Peru 153–1387 m (500–4,500 ft)	Carries larvae in a skin pouch on lower back.
P. bolivianus	26 mm (1 in)	Colour of living specimens unknown; preserved specimen brown with granulated back.	Bolivia: Amazon area 800–1,200 m (2,500–4,000 ft)	Rare species.
P. boulengeri	20 mm (¾ in)	Brown with spots. Light stripes across back.	Colombia to north-west Ecuador 10–1,145 m (30–4,750 ft)	Previously included in *Colostethus* by Savage.
P. espinosai	16–22 mm (⅝–⅞ in)	Back red. Flanks, belly, and thighs patterned.	Colombia: Chocó region 300–500 m (1,000–1,600 ft)	Small, very fast species of the damp forests.
P. ingeri	27 mm (1 in)	Colour of living specimens unknown; preserved examples black with white spots in armpits	Colombia: Caqueta 400 m (1,300 ft)	Only one specimen in existence.

Species	Size	Appearance	Distribution	Special features
P. petersi	28 mm (1⅛ in)	Skin granulated. Back brown, with yellow, white, or green lateral stripes	Peru, west of the eastern Andes 274–800 m (900–2,600 ft)	Belongs to *P. pictus* group.
P. pulchripectus	27 mm (1 in)	Back black, strongly granulated, with yellow lateral stripes. Belly blue-black, marbled.	Northern Brazil: Rio Amapari 100–310 m (300–1,000 ft)	Known only from this area.
P. smaragdinus	26.5 mm (1 in)	Black with green stripes across back. Belly blue or green.	Peru, east of the Andes. Venezuela: Pan de Azucar 360–380 m (1,200–1,250 ft)	Known only from this area.
P. zaparo	27–29 mm (1–1⅛ in)	Back red with white to light blue lateral stripes. Belly black.	Ecuador, east of the Andes 230–1,000 m (750–3,250 ft)	Largest species of *P. femoralis* group.

12

The Genus *Colostethus*

Colostethus inguinalis   Panama rocket frog   (Plate 50)

A number of species of false poison-arrow frogs or rocket frogs exist in Central and South America. Like the true poison-arrow frogs of the genera *Dendrobates* and *Phyllobates* they belong to the Dendrobatidae family. They do not secrete skin toxins, but their behaviour and breeding habits gives them the right to be considered as members of this highly specialized frog family. Only four of the more than seventy known species are discussed here, but this is enough to give an overall picture of the genus, *Colostethus*, to which they belong, because all the species, in their appearance and behaviour, have much in common.

Description *C. inguinalis* can attain a length of 32–34 mm (1¼–1⅜ in). It is very robust, with especially well-developed back legs. These enable it to live up to its name of rocket frog by reacting at great speed and with enormous leaps. Its colouring is brown to grey. On each dark brown flank is a short, light-coloured stripe running from the middle of the body to the groin. The extremities have dark cross bands, the belly is light coloured. Females are bigger than the males and have a lighter colouring.

Distribution and habitat Panama rocket frogs are found from Panama to Colombia. They live along streams and rivers in the lowland and up to 1,000 m (3,300 ft) above sea level. In suitable habitats they live in great numbers. I was able to observe them in their natural habitat in the high valley of El Valle in Panama. I found the frogs along a fast-flowing mountain stream, its waters rushing between huge boulders and fallen tree trunks to the valley below. Males defending their territories against neighbouring competitors, with loud calls, were sitting around on many of the huge rocks jutting up out of the water. When

A terrarium for the rocket frogs of the genus *C.* should include a running stream powered by a motor with a filter. A flower pot, with a piece broken away to form an entrance, may be placed at the edge of the stream. It will be used by the frogs for mating.

threatened they dived head first into the water and let the current carry them to the safety of another rock. Because they move so fast, these frogs are not easy to catch – and you need considerable acrobatic skill to negotiate the slippery rocks without tripping up. I found tadpoles in water at a relatively cool 20°C which also harboured a few attractive carp, probably of the genus *Fundulus*.

Care in the terrarium For these water-loving frogs the terrarium should be made to resemble a river bank, so it should have a pump-driven stream about 10 cm (4 in) deep, with a few large stones protruding slightly above the surface of the water. The males will adopt these stone islands as calling places. Depending on the place of origin of the rocket frogs, the water temperature should be between 18° and 24°C and the air temperature between 20° and 28°C.

The male initiates mating, coaxing a female to come to him and leading her to the prospective spawning place, which can consist of a smooth stone shaded by a root. The pair will be quite happy, though, with a clay-pot spawning house. The clutch consists of 20 to 30 eggs from which ready-to-hatch tadpoles will develop within 12 to 14 days. During this period only the female will guard the clutch and she will transfer the larvae to water. She squats on the gelatinous membranes until all the tadpoles have climbed on to her back and then sets out to find a suitable pool of water for the larvae, for example, a basin of water on the floor of the terrarium. She will give the young no further care.

The tadpoles should be transferred to an aquarium with a volume of about 30 l (6½ gal). The larvae are peaceable so they can be raised together. To ensure that the water is always clean and well oxygenated an aquarium filter should be used. There should be a few, preferably free-floating, water plants in the tank, so that the tadpoles will be able to find hiding places and places to rest.

Raising the larvae is not difficult. As omnivores they will accept algae, fish food, defrosted gnat larvae, and other foods. They reach metamorphosis in eight to ten weeks. At this point at the very latest some islands of cork oak should be floated on the water so that the newly transformed frogs can reach dry land. The young frogs will be about 1.2 cm (½ in) long at first. They should be fed on springtails and small *Drosophila* dusted with mineral powder. On a good diet they will reach adulthood in just under a year.

Colostethus saulii Rocket frog   (Plate 51)

Description *C. saulii* is a medium-sized species in which the females attain a length of 25 to 28 mm (1 to 1⅛ in); the males remain smaller at 22 mm (⅞ in). *C. saulii* is one of the more conspicuously coloured species of its genus. Its head is red-brown. Its back is black, with two red-brown lateral stripes. The legs are medium grey, with black cross bands. The throat and belly are light grey, and a short light-coloured stripe decorates the flanks. The toes, like those of all Dendrobatidae, are flattened into pads. The males have a vocal sac about the size of a pea, which makes it possible for them to project their chirping call, rather like that of a cricket, over quite a distance.

Distribution and habitat *C. saulii* lives in Peru, in the lowlands as well as in medium-high regions. It is concentrated in areas of vegetation-rich gravel along the courses of rivers. The frogs tend to sit on large stones washed by river water, into which they will dive at any sign of danger.

Care in the terrarium A terrarium for this water-loving frog should be set up as a river bank. My own group, of two females and two males, lives with two pairs of *P. tricolor* in a terrarium measuring 60 × 60 × 40 cm (2 × 2 × 1⅓ ft). To ensure high relative humidity, of 80 to 100 per cent, I installed a waterfall which bubbles over pieces of cork and stones. The frogs love to seek out spots gently washed by water – the males use them as calling stations. Temperatures should lie between 20° and 26°C.

Behaviour and breeding Like all Dendrobatidae, rocket frogs care for their young. Mating is initiated by a territory-owning male, which will first find a suitable calling station in his own territory. This station may well turn out to be also the later spawning space – indeed, quite often the male will call from the entrance of a spawning house. Beginning early in the morning he sits in front of the spawning house and calls almost without interruption, making chirping sounds lasting several seconds. His pea-sized vocal sac swells up greatly, amplifying his calls so that they can be heard many yards away. When a female approaches he becomes more excited – his calls become even louder, he shakes all over, and he changes colour so that he seems almost black. As the female comes closer he moves jerkily backwards and forwards and dances in circles, calling all the time. The female then follows him to the entrance of the spawning house and both disappear inside. From then on it can take hours until the female spawns. Sometimes the male will remain in the spawning house too, but sometimes he will go out for a while. During mating the pair will clasp one another even outside the spawning house – the male hops on to the female's back and grabs her around the throat with his front legs – but this lasts only for a few minutes.

The clutches produced by my frogs – which were still very young – have been of 12 to 16 eggs. The male minds the clutch and keeps it moist. He is an attentive guardian and during the development period, which lasts anything between one and twelve days, he spends most of the day looking after the clutch, chasing other frogs from the vicinity by jumping on them or generally shoving them about. When the larvae hatch he carries them piggyback to water.

Raising larvae and young frogs The tadpoles can be reared quite easily. At first they will eat algae and micro-organisms, later on dried food and gnat larvae. They can be kept together, as they are quite sociable, but keeping more than six to eight tadpoles per litre of water is to be avoided, otherwise the weaker tadpoles will be retarded in growth – it seems that the larger tadpoles exude growth-inhibiting substances that are absorbed by the weaker ones if the population density is too high. The front legs erupt when the tadpoles are about seven weeks old and have attained a length of 30 mm (1⅛ in). A few days later the young frogs, now having a length of 10 mm (⅜ in) to begin with, will climb on land. They can be fed with the smallest food insects such as mites, springtails, small *Drosophila*, and freshly hatched field crickets. After about nine months in the terrarium they will attain adulthood.

Colostethus talamancae   Talamanca rocket frog   (Plate 52)

Description *C. talamancae* is one of the smaller rocket frogs. The females attain a length of 25 mm (1 in), the males remain somewhat smaller. They have a fairly modest colouring – the dark brown back has a simple beige-brown lateral stripe on either side. These dorso-lateral stripes run from the eyes to the back legs, where they may merge. The legs are more interesting in colour; light brown with dark bands and stripes and the back legs particularly may bear orange-red patterns. The belly is dark in males and light-coloured in females.

Distribution and habitat According to Schulte (1980) *C. talamancae* lives in Costa Rica, Panama, Colombia, and Ecuador, mainly in the lowlands, but also up to 750 m (2,500 ft) above sea level. The frogs are found near rivers and streams, but are not as fond of water as *C. inguinalis*. On Bastimentos in the Bocas Islands I found *C. talamancae* in a gently rising area of forest with a high degree of humidity on the ground. Small streamlets of water trickled down between luxuriant vegetation consisting of creepers and leafy plants. In this habitat we also discovered *Phyllobates lugubris*.

Care in the terrarium *C. talamancae*'s behaviour in a terrarium is quieter than that of *C. inguinalis*, so it can be kept in a smaller terrarium. The interior set-up can be much as for *C. inguinalis*, but *C. talamancae* will be content with a much smaller body of water. Otherwise there are no great differences between these two species with respect to behaviour and reproduction.

Colostethus trinitatis

Description At a length of up to 35 mm (1⅜ in), *C. trinitatis* is one of the larger rocket frogs. Colourwise it is not particularly interesting – it is a modest brown without conspicuous markings. The belly is white. The yellow throat of the females is the only notable colour feature. (The males have black throats, so the sexes can be distinguished quite easily.)

Distribution and habitat *C. trinitatis* inhabits northern South America, especially Venezuela, and can be found, too, on the Islands under the Wind off the Venezuelan coast, on Trinidad, and on Tobago. Like most of the rocket frogs, it is dependent on running water and in suitable habitats is quite numerous.

Care in the terrarium A suitable terrarium for rocket frogs should always be fashioned to resemble a river bank, as already described for *C. inguinalis*. Under suitable conditions the male begins the mating process by emitting constant whistling sounds. These frogs have been observed in their natural habitat on the island of Tobago. They were found beside shady streams, which provided them with hiding places in the form of stones or abandoned crab burrows, and were successfully bred when small clay pots were placed as spawning houses in a terrarium. The clutches were of 22 to 29 eggs, and caring for the larvae presented no problems. After about 60 days the larvae reach metamorphosis. The young frogs are 12 mm (½ in) long at first.

Other species of *Colostethus*

Species	Size	Appearance	Distribution	Special features
C. abditaurantius	27–30 mm (1–1⅛ in)	Head and back dark grey, white lateral spots. Back slightly granulated. Orange spots in armpits and groin. Throat and belly white.	Colombia: Cordillera Central, Bello (Antioquia) 1,450 m (4,750 ft)	For highlands type, temperatures around 20°C. Signal spots. Well-developed webbing on feet.
C. fraterdanieli	20–27 mm (¾–1in)	Head and back light brown. Flanks dark brown with diagonal gold stripes. Belly yellowish to white. Skin smooth.	Colombia: Santa Rita 1,890–2,500 m (6,200–8,250 ft)	Lives in very high, cool mountain regions. Males have thickened third finger and black dotted throat.
C. imbricolus	28 mm (1⅛ in)	Head and back dark brown. Two faint gold stripes across back. Flanks black with a gold stripe. Throat and belly black with numerous blue spots.	Colombia: Alto de Buey, Chocó region 1,070 m (3,500 ft)	Orange signal spots around the armpits, thighs, and calves. Webbed toes. Stripes across back.
C. lehmanni	20 mm (¾ in)	Head and back brown. Flanks brown with white spots and gold lateral stripes. Skin mainly smooth.	Colombia: Santa Rita 1,890–1,910 m (6,200–6,250 ft)	Highland type which lives on very damp forest floor amid numerous bromeliads and mosses at average temperatures around 20°C (minimum 10°C, maximum 30°C) and average annual precipitation 5,000 mm (200 in).

Species	Size	Appearance	Distribution	Special features
C. nubicola	22 mm (⅞ in)	Back dark brown. Flanks black. Back and flank patterns separated by a narrow, light stripe. Belly white to light yellow.	Costa Rica. Panama 0–1,800 m (0–6,000 ft)	Different temperature requirements according to region of origin. Males have dark spotted throat and thickened third digit.
C. ramosi	20 mm (¾ in)	Head and back dark brown. Flanks black with gold diagonal stripes. Skin smooth.	Colombia: Alto de la Honda 1,240 m (4,000 ft)	Small highland type which lives in leaf litter, not tied to large bodies of water. Temperatures around 23°C. Males have black patterned throats.

Bibliography

Bechter, R., 'Das Ei des Kolumbus (Zur Aufzucht von *Dendrobates pumilio* und *lehmanni*)', *Aquarien-Magazin*, **6**, 1978, pp. 272–6.

Bechter, R. and J. Lescure, '*Dendrobates quinquevittatus*: Fortpflanzungsverhalten im Terrarium und Vielgestaltigkeit der Art (Teil 2)', *Herpetofauna*, **22**, 1983, pp. 28–32.

Beutelschiess, J. and C., '*Dendrobates speciosus* – ein Rubin im Terrarium', *Herpetofauna*, **5** (25), 1983, pp. 6–8.

Friederich, U. and W. Volland, *Futtertierzucht*, Verlag Eugen Ulmer, Stuttgart, Germany, 1981.

Graeff, D. and R. Schulte, 'Neue Erkenntnisse zur Brutbiologie von *Dendrobates pumilio*, *Herpetofauna*, **7**, 1980, pp. 17–22.

Heselhaus, R., *Pfeilgiftfrösche*, Reimar Hobbing Verlag, Edition Kernen, Essen, Germany, 1984.

— *Taggeckos*, Reimar Hobbing Verlag, Edition Kernen, Essen, Germany, 1986.

— *Laubfrösche im Terrarium*, Reimar Hobbing Verlag, Edition Kernen, Essen, Germany, 1987a.

— ' "Streichholzvorderbeine" bei Dendrobatiden-Nachzuchten', *Die Aquarien- und Terrarienzeitschrift*, **10**, 1987b, pp. 466–8.

Kneller, M., 'Die Fortpflanzung von *Dendrobates reticulatus* im natürlichen Lebensraum und im Terrarium', *Das Aquarium*, **3**, 1982a, pp. 148–51.

— 'Erfolgreiche Nachzucht des Blauen Pfeilgiftfrösches *Dendrobates azureus*', *Herpetofauna*, **19**, 1982b, pp. 6–9.

— 'Beobachtungen an *Dendrobates fantasticus* im natürlichen Lebensraum und im Terrarium', *Herpetofauna*, **24**, 1983, pp. 15–18.

Kneller, M. and K. Henle, 'Ein neuer Blattsteiger-Frosch (Salienta: Dendrobatidae: Phyllobates) aus Peru', *Salamandra*, **21** (1), 1985, pp. 62–9.

Myers, C. W., 'Spotted poison frogs: Descriptions of three new *Dendrobates* from western Amazonia, and resurrection of a lost species from "Chiriquí" ', *American Museum of Natural History*, **2721**, 1982, pp. 1–23, figs. 1–12.

Myers, C. W. and J. W. Daly, 'A new species of poison frog (*Dendrobates*) from Andean Ecuador, including an analysis of its skin toxins', *Occasional Papers of the Museum of Natural History, University of Kansas*, **59**, 1976, pp. 1–12.

— 'A name for the poison frog of Cordillera Azul, eastern Peru, with notes on its biology and skin toxins (Dendrobatidae)', *American Museum of Natural History*, **2674**, 1979.

— 'Taxonomy and ecology of *Dendrobates bombetes*, a new Andean poison frog with new skin toxins', *American Museum of Natural History*, **2692**, 1980.

— 'Dart-poison frogs', *Scientific American*, **248** (2), 1983a, pp. 120–33.

— 'Pfeilgiftfrösche', *Spektrum der Wissenschaft*, 4, 1983b, pp. 34–43.

Myers, C.W., J. W. Daly and B. Malkin, 'A dangerously toxic new frog (*Phyllobates*) used by Emberá Indians of western Colombia, with discussion of blowgun fabrication and dart poisoning', *Bulletin of American Museum of Natural History*, **161** (2), 1978.

Myers, C. W., J. W. Daly, B. Malkin and V. Martinez, 'An arboreal poison frog (*Dendrobates*) from western Panama', *American Museum of Natural History*, **2692**, 1980.

Nietzke, G., *Fortpflanzung und Aufzucht der Terrarientiere*, Landbuch Verlag, Hanover, Germany, 1984.

Rauh, W., *Bromeliad Lexicon*, Blandford, London, 1990.

Schlüter, A., 'Die Froschlurche an einem Stillgewässer im tropischen Regenwald von Peru', *Herpetofauna*, **9** (47), 1987, pp. 11–20.

Schmidt, M., 'Variantenreich ist der Goldbaumsteiger (*Dendrobates auratus*)', *Das Aquarium*, **221**, 1987, pp. 592–4.

Schulte, R., '*Dendrobates silverstonei*, ein neuer Giftfrosch aus Peru', *Herpetofauna*, **1**, 1979, pp. 24–30.

— *Frösche und Kroten*, Verlag Eugen Ulmer, Stuttgart, Germany, 1980.

— '*Dendrobates bassleri* – Freilandbeobachtungen, Haltung und Zucht', *Herpetofauna*, **12**, 1981, pp. 23–8.

— 'Eine neue *Dendrobates*-Art aus Ostperu. (Amphibien: Salientia: Dendrobatidae)', *Sauria*, **8** (3), 1986, pp. 11–20.

Silverstone, P. A., 'Status of certain frogs of genus *Colostethus*, with descriptions of new species', *Los Angeles County Museum*, **215**, 1971.

— 'A revision of the poison-arrow frogs of the genus *Dendrobates* Wagler', *Scientific Bulletin of the Natural History Museum of Los Angeles*, **21**, 1975a, pp. 1–55.

— 'Two new species of *Colostethus* from Colombia', *Natural History Museum of Los Angeles*, **268**, 1975b.

— 'A revision of poison-arrow frogs of the genus *Phyllobates* bibron in Sagra (family Dendrobatidae)', *Scientific Bulletin of the Natural History Museum of Los Angeles*, **27**, 1976, pp. 1–53.

Stettler, P. H., *Handbuch der Terrarienkunde*, Kosmos/Franckh'sche Verlagshandlung, Stuttgart, Germany, 1978.

Weygoldt, P., 'Durch Nachzucht erhalten: Der Färberfrosch *Dendrobates tinctorius*', *Aquarien-Magazin*, **1**, 1982, pp. 6–13.

— 'Durch Nachzucht erhalten: Blattsteigerfrösche (Drei Arten aus der *Phyllobates-pictus*-Gruppe)', *Aquarien-Magazin*, **11**, 1983, pp. 566–72.

Zimmermann, H., *Tropische Frösche*, Kosmos/Franckh'sche Verlagshandlung, Stuttgart, Germany, 1978.

— 'Verhaltensbeobachtungen an Färberfröschen', *Aquarien-Magazin*, **9**, 1978, pp. 458–63.

— *Das Züchten von Terrarientieren*, Kosmos/Franckh'sche Verlagshandlung, Stuttgart, Germany, 1983.

Zimmermann, H. and E., 'Durch Nachzucht erhalten: Färberfrösche (*Dendrobates histrionicus* und *D. lehmanni*)', *Aquarien-Magazin*, **10**, pp. 562–9.

— 'Durch Nachzucht erhalten: Baumsteigerfrösche (*Dendrobates quinquevittatus* und *D. reticulatus*)', *Aquarien-Magazin*, **1**, 1984, pp. 35–41.

— 'Der Gelbe Pfeilgiftfrosch – der "Schreckliche" (Verhalten und Pflege)', *Aquarien-Magazin*, **10**, 1985a, pp. 424–7.

— 'Durch Nachzucht erhalten: Der Gelbe Pfeilgiftfrosch', *Aquarien-Magazin*, **11**, 1985b, pp. 460, 463.

— 'Zur Situation der Baumsteiger- oder Pfeilgiftfrösche (Familie Dendrobatidae) in der Natur sowie zu ihrer Artenerhaltung durch Zucht und ihrem Schutz durch Gesetze', *Herpetofauna*, **9** (49), 1987, pp. 31–4.

Index

Amphibia 11
Antibiotics 49
Atopophrynus 12

Batrachotoxin 29, 31
Behaviour; *see also* Territory 35, 66, 70, 77, 92, 96, 103
Blow-pipe dart 29, 81, 89
Bocas Islands 19, 21, 86
Bone rot 49
Breeding 53–55
   in a terrarium 44, 47, 58, 66, 70, 77, 90, 92, 96, 103
Bromeliad 42, 53, 55, 60, 63, 72, 74, 75, 77
   fields 24, 27
   vases 14, 54, 71

Classification 12
Colostethus 12, 13, 18
   abditaurantius 106
   fraterdanieli 106
   imbricolus 106
   inguinalis 18, 68, 100, 104, 105
   lehmanni 106
   nubicola 106
   ramosi 106
   saulii 102
   talamancae 86, 104
   trinitatis 105
Crickets
   field 46, 67, 76, 77, 90, 93, 98, 104
   house 46, 76, 77, 85, 87, 90, 93, 98

Dendrobates 12, 54
   abditus 79
   altobueyensis 68, 79
   arboreus 79
   auratus 15, 16, 17, 20, 52, 56–58, 66
   azureus 58
   bombetes 79
   captivus 79
   fantasticus 59, 62, 74
   femoralis 24, 84

fulguritus 68, 79
galactonotus 79
granuliferus 37, 61
histrionicus 37, 54, 55, 61, 62, 64
imitator 60, 62, 63, 74
lehmanni 37, 64
leucomelas 65, 78
maculatus 80
minutus 19, 68
mysteriosus 80
opisthomelas 68, 80
pumilio 11, 19, 20, 21, 22, 31, 32, 33, 36, 37, 51, 53, 54, 55, 58, 61, 69–71, 76, 77, 86
quinquevittatus 13, 24, 25, 34, 37, 51, 54, 55, 60, 62, 63, 64, 68, 71, 74, 75
reticulatus 60, 62, 72, 74
speciosus 37, 55, 76
silverstonei 14, 29, 75
steyermarki 68, 80
tinctorius 26, 31, 58, 77
truncatus 80
vanzolinii 80
Diet 44, 54
   specialists 55, 61
Diseases 48

El Valle 17, 68, 100
Embryo, development of 51
Epiphytes 42
Evolution 21, 22

French Guiana 23, 26, 71, 72
Food
   eggs 36, 37, 61
   insects 44, 60, 96
Fruit fly 45, 46, 50, 60, 66, 67, 69, 70, 71, 77, 85, 87, 89, 90, 93, 95, 97, 98, 104

Habitat 13, 16, 25, 34

Jungle islands 28, 58

'Meadow plankton' 45

Moths
  Indian Meal 46
  Wax 47, 66, 87, 90, 93
Mutation 22, 34

Nomenclature, 11

Panama 15, 56, 69
Panama rocket frog 100
Parental care 36
Phyllobates 12, 54
  anthonyi 12, 85, 98
  aurotaenia 29, 30, 81, 83, 89
  azureiventris 81
  bassleri 12, 82
  bicolor 29, 30, 81, 83, 89, 90
  bolivianus 12, 98
  boulengeri 12, 85, 98
  espinosai 85, 98
  femoralis 12, 84, 87
  ingeri 12, 98
  lugubris 32, 58, 82, 83, 85, 96, 105
  parvulus 12, 87
  petersi 12, 87, 98
  pictus 12, 87
  pulchripectus 12, 87, 98
  smaragdinus 12, 98
  terribilis 29, 30, 31, 83, 84, 89
  tricolor 12, 31, 32, 50, 52, 66, 85, 88,
    92, 103

trivattatus 12, 95
vittatus 83, 85, 90, 96
zaparo 12, 85, 98
Pumilio toxin 29

Quarantine 48, 49

Reproduction 34, 55
Rocket frogs 17, 102

'Scratching disease' 49, 61
Skin toxin 87
Spindly-leg syndrome 50, 51, 53
Strawberry poison-dart frog 11, 19, 21,
  36, 37, 49, 51, 53, 55, 69–71

Taboga 56
Talamanca rocket frog 104
Taxonomy 11
Terrarium 31, 37–52
  the building of 38–40
  climate 38, 43, 44
  interior furnishing 40–42
Territory 32
Tobago 105
Toxins
  frogs' skin 29, 30, 31, 34, 81, 89
  use for darts 29, 89

UV light 43, 44